Little Cindy's Letters

Cindy Rogers & Robert Abel

Valentine Publishing House
Denver, Colorado

Valentine Publishing House LLC
P.O. Box 27422, Denver, Colorado 80227

Cover graphics by Desert Isle Design, LLC.

Publisher's Cataloging-in-Publication Data

Rogers, Cindy A.
Little Cindy's Letters / Cindy Rogers & Robert Abel.

p. ; cm.
ISBN: 0-9711536-2-0

1. Eating disorders—Religious aspects—Christianity. 2. Healing—Religious aspects—Christianity. 3. Spiritual life—Catholic church. 4. Anorexia nervosa. 5. Bulimia. I. Abel, Robert A. II. Title.

BX2373.S5 .R64 2005
248.86/25

2005920215

Printed in the United States of America.

"*Little Cindy's Letters,* an anointed book that shows us the power of love to heal any hurt and protect us against all evil."

— Michael Brown, SpiritDaily.Com

"I have just finished reading *Little Cindy's Letters* and found it fascinating. Already I plan to send it to several Catholic friends I know who are having problems with eating disorders. In addition to the profound healing techniques, this book shows how a prayer minister armed with spiritual insight can help others heal through the love and power of the risen Christ."

— Francis MacNutt, Christian Healing Ministries

"*Little Cindy's Letters* is a dynamic collection of healing letters that pierces the heart for Christ."

— Father Emmerich Vogt, O.P.

Chapter One

Hello,

I'm fighting a terrible food addiction. I picked up your book hoping to get help. Do you give retreats or have anything to help people? I love the Catholic faith and the Blessed Mother, and I desperately want to be free from this food addiction. Can you help me?

— Cindy

Dear Cindy,

Sure, I will help you. Have you read my book on spiritual warfare yet? Do you have any questions? I would like you to look at your childhood wounds. Try to get in touch with the five-year-old girl from your past. What does she have to say?

— Rob

Dear Rob,

Thank you. It was very kind of you to respond to my request. I'm in the process of reading your book. I really don't remember much about my childhood except that it was extremely painful, with tremendous verbal abuse.

I can't remember being five. I've tried before. I'll be 51 tomorrow, and I've spent a lot of years pushing those memories down. What I do remember is very painful. I always felt like a failure and a reject, and that nobody could possibly love me, and that I could never do anything right. It's hard for me to talk about this, but I'm willing to do anything to get help.

I was always extremely thin, and at one time, I was treated for anorexia. Now I'm extremely obese. I do everything in extremes. I hate myself and don't know how God could love somebody like me. My life is out of control. I'm fighting my own demons with this food addiction, and I can't seem to dig my way out of this messy house.

We are building a new house and going to be moving in a few weeks. I wish I could just walk away, start over and leave it all behind. I don't want to take all this baggage with me — literally and figuratively.

— Cindy

Dear Cindy,

I think leaving it all behind is an excellent idea. Why not go through your house and get rid of everything you have not used in the last few years? Many people have a tendency to save stuff just in case they need it in the future, but if you haven't used something in the last two years, what's the chance you will *ever* use it?

I try to live very simply. I go through my belongings on a regular basis to look for anything I can throw out. Last month, I threw out a bagful of cassette tapes. I don't need them, will never use them and would rather feel light and free.

After completing a little work on your exterior environment, why not start a little internal house cleaning? I would like to see you write 50 positive affirmations about yourself. Just send me the list when you're finished.

It will be very powerful for you to read this list out loud several times a day. It will counteract the tremendous verbal abuse that you have suffered. After you have completed this first assignment, I will show you how to dig down deep into your heart and heal all your traumatic past experiences. Afterwards you will be totally free — free to be the woman of God the Lord created you to be.

— Rob

Dear Rob,

I do intend to start pitching things, but if you could see my house, you would know this is not going to be easy. It all feels so overwhelming, but I will do what you have asked, one pile at a time. I don't think I'm up to writing the list of affirmations yet. I really can't think of anything good to say about myself.

I wanted to ask you how to stop feeling so overwhelmed, because I end up turning to food for comfort. I don't know how to stop doing it. A part of me wants to stop eating, yet another part of me doesn't. I hope you understand.

— Cindy

Dear Cindy,

Here's the secret weapon that you have been waiting for: the battle needs to be fought one victory at a time. You have enough power, strength and energy to get up, take a pile of newspapers to the trash can and throw them out. Afterwards, say to yourself, I don't need these. I don't need anything but Jesus! Then find a way to love yourself and feel good about throwing the newspapers away. Find a way to give yourself the love, safety and security that the newspapers were providing.

That's where the list of positive affirmations comes in. By affirming and loving the hurt part of yourself, you will have less of a need to acquire and consume stuff. The stuff you eat to make yourself feel better and the stuff you acquire around your house is a false god. It will never fill the void deep within your soul. It will always leave you wanting more. It will never heal you.

Please send me five affirmations. You have the power to send me five right now. Send me five, and I will send you five more in return. One victory at a time! Send over your list and allow yourself to feel good about the accomplishment.

How about being courageous? You must be a woman of great courage to reach out for help. And strength! It takes great strength to make yourself vulnerable. Say that to yourself over and over again. Start giving yourself the love that you need by saying, *I am a woman of great strength and courage! I am a woman of great strength and courage!* Now say it a hundred times out loud and mean it. Say it in such a way that it brings your heavenly Father to tears.

— Rob

Dear Rob,

Thank you for saying those kind words to me yesterday. You're right about the stuff. I have read your letter over and over. Just last night, I was able to throw some stuff away and start a bag to give to the poor. It wasn't easy, but I did it. And even harder, I wanted to eat all night. Like an alcoholic wants a drink, I wanted to go get food. I made myself stay in the bedroom all night and not go near the kitchen. This went on all night!

I just couldn't believe the answer starts with one victory at a time. Wow! I can't believe how much your words got through to me. You have reached out to a soul who has been drowning for many years. I know that this is going to be a constant and ongoing battle, and that this is just the beginning, but I feel as though I fought my first battle last night, and this morning I feel stronger.

I'm so grateful to you for helping me. I can hardly write this because of all the tears. I have been asking every priest on every corner and in every confessional for help for many years. I have been praying and praying, and finally God answered my prayers with your letter and it got me through the first battle. I feel like a little baby who has just taken her first step.

— Cindy

I'm a servant of the Lord.
I want to do God's will in my life.
I'm a loving wife and mother.
I love the Catholic faith.
I am a child of the light.

Dear Cindy,

I wanted to send you five more affirmations to match the five you sent over, but after thinking about your situation, I realized the solution needs to come from inside your heart.

God is calling you deep into your heart. He wants to meet you there. He knows your pain. He feels your pain. He longs to heal you. He wants you, all of you. He is calling you on an exciting adventure deep into your soul. It's an adventure of a lifetime. Just you and the Lover of your soul on a passionate journey, through many tears — a great adventure into your past.

You were hurt as a little girl and traumatized. The Lord's heart breaks for you, for the hurt and scared little girl who lives inside of you. She longs to be loved. She is very lonely. She is calling out to you. Please take Jesus' hand and visit this hurt little girl from your past. She needs you. She loves you.

I can only show you the door: it is deep inside your heart. Please do whatever it takes to go there. Share with me what you find, but most importantly, love that little girl, find her, she is calling out to you, she needs you! Find her and love her with all your strength. She is incredible, beautiful and precious in the eyes of God.

— Rob

Chapter Two

Dear Rob,

Nothing short of a miracle is happening. You must really be praying! I haven't binged for three days! I know it's just a start and it's only been three days, but I'm feeling a strength that I have never felt before.

Now, about this little girl thing: I'm going to do what you say, but I'm scared to try it because I know it will be really hard and painful. Did you ask the Lord about this little girl thing? Did the Lord want you to say that to me, or is this coming from your psychiatrist training?

I know I'm at the bottom of a very high mountain that I have to climb. For the first time in my life, I feel that I will make it to the top. I'll feel so much better when I get there. Before, I didn't think I could make it; now I think I can. Thank you so much, from the bottom of my heart!

— Cindy

Dear Cindy,

I need to be thanking you. I have over a hundred biblical affirmations that I could have sent over, but the Spirit wasn't prompting me to send anything except the words I wrote.

When I started to write you the last letter, all of a sudden the tears hit me. All I could feel was deep compassion from the Lord. I cried for five minutes writing those words about little Cindy. There was a pile of toilet paper that I had used to blow my nose sitting on my desk afterwards.

Those words I wrote to you are spirit and truth directly from the Source. I haven't cried in months. The last time I cried was at Easter, and I barely shed a tear. I was just happy to hear a pastor that I like preach. I think you need to read that letter over and over again until is cuts through any hardness of heart. Evil doesn't want you to get inside your heart.

It was totally God and, wow, he has great love for you. Give it a try. What do you have to lose? Take the letter, and Jesus, and go deep inside your heart, embrace little Cindy, and you will see what I'm talking about. Don't wait. Do it now when you're strong. You have just had three days of non-bingeing victory. Do it now in the peak of your strength.

Take a blanket and some tissues with you. Find a safe, secure place in your home where the Lord can show you and little Cindy his incredible love. Keep pursuing her until you're moved by the same tears of compassion that I have cried on your behalf.

— Rob

Dear Rob,

I was doing really well until last night when I lost it and binged. The urge was so strong I couldn't fight back. I've been thinking more about little Cindy than I have in years, trying to go back and relive experiences with the Lord. I have cried many tears and felt a lot of pain, but I can't seem to go back past the eighth grade.

There's so much hurt from the eighth grade to high school. My parents put me in a mental institution when I was 15 for trying to commit suicide. The abuse that happened there was unbelievable. I don't know if I'm doing this right, but I'm trying. I feel that the doors, which have stood between the Lord and me, are coming down. I'm crying just to write that.

I want so much to be close to him and feel his love for me, but I feel very undeserving. I'm trying to lose that attitude and let his love, which I know in my head, flow into my heart. I want to have a close and personal relationship with him. I know him on one level, but I don't let him love me.

I'm trying to put my journal time with the Lord as a top priority. I have to write to keep my mind focused. Even though it's difficult and very painful, I will keep working at it.

— Cindy

Dear Cindy,

If you can't get in touch with five-year-old Cindy, go back and love teenage Cindy.

I'm glad to hear you like to journal, because I want to ask you to journal every day for the next ten days in front of the Blessed Sacrament. Focus on teenage Cindy. Allow her to vent her anger, frustration and shame on paper. Every day, pick a different situation that she has suffered and work through all the negative emotions on paper.

After you have completed the venting part, you will need to replace those negative emotions with positive, loving emotions. Turn the page and start speaking loving, compassionate words to teenage Cindy. Allow God to speak to her through your writing. On God's behalf, write down all the loving words that Jesus would say to that hurt and scared little girl.

Start out with, "I'm sorry you were hurt. You didn't deserve to be treated like that. I was there with you. I hurt when you were hurt. I love you. I see your beauty."

— Rob

Dear Rob,

I think I'm doing something wrong. I think I'm able to go back and dig up too much hurt. I'm opening the wound really wide, and I don't know how to take the Lord with me, not even in front of the Blessed Sacrament.

I have never felt worse or more alone in all my life. I don't feel the Lord's comfort in the situation and all I'm doing is opening these wounds big-time. I feel more attacked by the devil than ever! I'm going to be 300 pounds before this is over.

My self-esteem is down in the gutter as deep as it can get. I'm embarrassed to leave my house. My son's in high school, and it's so hard to go to his games. I know it's pride, but it's really hard. I want to be there for him, but when I come home, I want to eat away the pain.

It's killing me! I don't feel like I can take another bite to stuff down the pain. I can't get it down anymore, yet I eat and eat and eat. I can't stop. I can hear the devil laughing at me when I'm doing it, and yet I can't stop.

I feel like I'm lying on the side of the road bleeding, and I will surely die. I can't even tell anybody this, because I'm so ashamed. It's like I'm pretending to be another person. I've spent years trying to be somebody else, always afraid that if my family and friends saw the real me, they would all leave.

Please, don't be mad at me. I'm disappointed enough for both of us. It's the hardest thing in the world to say all this to another person. I'm afraid if I don't bring everything to the light, Satan will use it against me.

— Cindy

Dear Cindy,

If you dig up all the hurt at once and put yourself through extreme mental anguish and then binge afterwards, it won't work. A healing letter can be a profound encounter with the Lord's love. I have actually felt 20 pounds lighter the day after a powerful healing experience.

I would like to work through one experience at a time. Please pick one really bad experience that happened to little Cindy or teenage Cindy and send it to me. Try to isolate the experience. I don't want to see all the bad stuff that happened to you over a five-year period — just one event, at one time.

Allow teenage Cindy to share all her anger, shame, guilt, fear and sadness regarding this bad experience. Allow her to pour her heart out.

Afterwards, you and I will respond back to her.

I want you, the adult Cindy, to keep out of it. I don't want to see you rationalize anything or intellectually control or interfere with the situation. I don't even want you to proofread it or correct grammar or spelling. Little Cindy has the right to spell any way she wants to.

I know you were hurt, little Cindy, and I'm here to listen. I want to hear what you have to say. You can trust me. I will help you.

— Rob

Dear Rob,

My parents sent me to the Salvation Army in another town. It was not a good place. It was more like a prison than a place of love. It was a home for unwed mothers, and they sure made me feel like a sinner.

I was sent there to have a child out of wedlock. I was so scared and all alone. I wanted to keep my baby, but my family wouldn't let me come home if I did. Even though I didn't want to be pregnant at this time, I wanted this baby more than life itself. I felt so alone and scared. I didn't think I would live through it, mentally or physically.

During delivery, I heard them say that the baby was breech and the cord was wrapped around its neck and it wasn't breathing. They called for more doctors and help, and I remember saying to God, "If you let this baby live, I'll give it a mother and father to give it the kind of life it deserves."

I didn't find out until later that it was a girl, and I never got to see her. They had taken the child out of the room, but from a distance, after I said that prayer, I heard a cry. I knew then she would be OK.

I have never felt so empty or incredibly sad my whole life. I really didn't want to live. I just remember lying in the recovery room alone for what seemed like hours. I was crying for my parents, but they weren't there. They weren't even in the same state with me. They told everybody the baby died during childbirth.

I can still feel the emptiness and longing for my baby. There's no greater loss ever to be had by a mother. I thought I had to give her up. It didn't feel like I had a choice. I gave her up so she could have the kind of home every child deserves. I went home a couple days later, and my parents never talked about it again.

I cried myself to sleep every night for weeks. I knew that nothing could ever fill the hole that was made in my heart that night. From that day forward, I decided that except for murdering somebody, I had committed the biggest sin possible, and that my punishment for all eternity was to never have or hold or see my baby again.

The next day, the people who adopted my baby came with their attorney and brought me a check. They said they wanted me to have it for a new start. I started crying hysterically. I tore it up in front of them and said, "I will never sell my baby!" Then the attorney made me sign a paper.

The next day, I wanted my baby back. I even tried to get her back days and months later, but nobody would tell me anything. I tried so hard to find out from everybody, but nobody would tell me anything.

I have never felt so much pain and loss, before or since. All I wanted that dark night were my parents, but they weren't there. I have been trying for 32 years to push down the hurt, pain, loss and shame. I felt so worthless that I could never forgive myself for what I had done, and nothing could ever fill the hole that is now deep down inside of me.

I still feel it to this day. How could I ever be worth anything to anybody after committing this kind of transgression? The baby's father wanted nothing to do with me. I didn't even want me, and I was too afraid of hell to kill myself.

I have been sitting here in the dark crying and typing. It's hard for me to say all this to you. I have never said all this to anybody, but the Lord told me I could trust you.

— Cindy

Chapter Three

Good job, Cindy.

I want you to work on this scene until it's healed by using a combination of imagination and written techniques. Find a private place in your home where you can be alone and undisturbed. Bring some tissues, a blanket and whatever else you need.

Start your imagination technique by getting comfortable. Release everything from your mind. Picture a beach scene, or a mountain setting, and allow yourself to feel the breeze, hear the tide and feel the sun on your face. Stay in this scene for about five minutes. This is your imagination, and you are in control. You can imagine any relaxing setting you want.

Next, picture a time machine. Picture adult Cindy, Jesus and me jumping into it and going for a ride into your past. We exit the time machine and arrive at the hospital. We walk through the automatic doors. You are in the middle, I'm on your left side, and Jesus is on your right.

Together we are a powerful force. As we walk down the halls, heading for teenage Cindy's room, the doctors and nurses clear out of our way. Many stagger backwards when they feel the Lord's presence.

After entering teenage Cindy's room, I want you to walk over and give her a hug. I know she is hurting, so I want you to tell her that we are here to comfort her. Tell her we will never leave her and that we love her. Tell her it's not her fault and that she didn't know any better.

I would like you to write and speak many encouraging words to teenage Cindy. Look her in the eyes, hold her and reassure her that she is doing the best she can.

Because this is your imagination, and you can do anything you want, I want you to invite your parents into the room. Imagine that Jesus worked a miracle and filled them with his love. I realize your parents were not filled with love at the time, but again, this is your imagination, and you have the freedom to work on it any way you want.

Have your parents enter the room and apologize to teenage Cindy. Have them state their apology with complete sincerity. Have them speak the words, "We are sorry. We were wrong. We should have helped you. We shouldn't have abandoned you. Please forgive us. We should have stood by you. We should have loved you. We should have listened to you. We didn't know better. Please forgive us."

After your parents say this, write down all the loving words that teenage Cindy deserves to hear. After you finish writing an apology letter on your parent's behalf, have Jesus walk over and forgive them before you send them back in the time machine.

Allow Jesus to take teenage Cindy into his arms and hold her. Have Jesus say, "Your sins are forgiven and you are washed clean. You are my little lamb. Please accept my forgiveness. Stop hurting yourself. It grieves me to see you so hurtful towards yourself."

After Jesus says anything else that teenage Cindy needs to hear, I want you to take her out of the hospital. Help her get dressed. Then have us all leave the room, walk down the hall and stop by the nursery. I want you to find your baby and allow teenage Cindy to pick her up and hold her.

After we leave the hospital, I want you to walk down the street to a beautiful white church. Picture all of us entering through the double doors and going inside. Please ask teenage Cindy if she feels at peace inside the church. Allow her to hold her baby for as long as she likes. When it's the right time, allow teenage Cindy to give her child to Jesus. Allow Jesus to hold and care for the baby girl. She belongs to him.

Whenever you are ready, say good-bye to teenage Cindy and leave her with Jesus inside the church. I want you to go over and over this scene in your imagination as many times as necessary. Work through it, and continue to work through it using different variations until teenage Cindy feels completely loved and at peace.

— Rob

Dear Rob,

Every time I go into the hospital room with teenage Cindy, I cry so hard I can hardly take it. All I can say to her is that I'm sorry. It still feels as though I did something wrong, like I sinned and I'm guilty.

Sure, my parents hurt me, but I hurt them, too. I broke the dream they had for me. This is what I'm having trouble dealing with. I can forgive everybody but myself. That's why I don't want to see Jesus. I'm too ashamed. That's why it's so hard to accept love from him, because I'm so undeserving.

I'm sorry. I'm really trying hard. Just reading your letter of what you want me to do continually brings the tears like you can't imagine. I'm here in the scene. I am teenage Cindy. I just lost my baby. I don't know how to comfort her, because I am still her. It's like time stood still with her and me. I can't do this.

— Cindy

Dear Rob,

Right after I wrote to you, Satan went into full swing. I haven't been able to sleep. Worry and anxiety have filled me to overflowing. Last night, I literally thought I was dying. I wrote to you out of desperation, but didn't want to give you any more to deal with, so I didn't send it. I felt so alone and frightened.

This morning, I feel like the biggest failure at everything, and the most hopeless case. I know this kind of thinking isn't from the Lord, but I couldn't seem to shake it, all night or all day. I can't live like this anymore.

I don't want to keep sinning by living in addiction mode, and I don't want to feel like I'm failing the Lord and my family. I look at myself, and I don't even know the person looking back at me. Why am I telling all this to you? I don't even know you. I feel as though you're not even a real person, more like an angel or something.

Today at Adoration, I had planned to spend some time doing what you told me to do, but had forgot to bring your letter with me. I couldn't remember how you said to do it, so I sat there and thought about the day I had my baby. I pictured you, me and Jesus walking down the hall together. That alone was extremely healing and let some love come into me. Now I'm sitting here bawling again, but it's helping.

I have never wanted to do this, because every time I tried with different people, I shut down with them because I didn't feel safe. This time I really do feel safe with you, but it's still so hard thinking about these things. I have spent my whole life trying not to think about them.

I will go back and reread the things you wanted me to say and do. I can still hardly breathe from all the darkness that enveloped me this week.

It won't be easy, but I don't want easy. I want healing. I don't want to be like this anymore. I feel stronger just knowing you are in my corner. I can only say thank you from the bottom of my heart. Hopefully, my next letter will have more good news to report.

— With love and gratitude, Cindy

Dear Cindy,

You are making great progress. I know it doesn't look or feel like you are improving, but I assure you, you are. This is the place where the battle takes place. All you have to do is seek the Lord with all your strength.

You are healing a major event in your life. I call those events big-ticket items. After you work through a big-ticket item, all kinds of freedom and blessings follow.

Healing is happening when you walked down the hospital hall with Jesus. More healing will occur when you write your parents' apology letter. If you are unable to write or accept your parents' apology, then you and the Lord will need to support and empower teenage Cindy with whatever she needs to work through it.

Let me know what's going on with teenage Cindy, and keep fighting with all your strength for freedom. Resist the devil, and it will flee from you! Keep seeking the Lord with all your heart, and he will deliver you.

— Rob

Dear Rob,

Just reading your response has helped me tremendously. I will eventually be able to come up with my own responses, and leave my baby with Jesus. Right now, all I can do is cry.

I can't even believe I'm doing this. I have spent my whole life trying not to think about this, but for some reason, just the fact of you and Jesus walking into the hospital with me has given me strength. Giving my baby to Jesus is better than giving my baby to an attorney, but all this is bringing so many tears. I suppose it's a good thing.

I feel so drained. I've been running for a long time. Now I realize, I was only running from the Lord, because I was afraid to face him and my sins. If I faced him, then I would have to do something about it. I kept saying I wanted to do better, but I was doing nothing to make that happen.

I would pray for the Lord to help me, but I refused to open the gifts of grace he was giving me. All my life I have run away from everything and everybody.

This morning I've been sitting here thinking how much I need the Lord. I don't want to run anymore. I want to face him and be with him. I love him. I need him desperately. Thank you for bringing me to this point.

— Cindy

Dear Rob,

Here's what I wrote last night to teenage Cindy:

You are like a little lamb surrounded by wolves who have devoured you. Jesus and I still love you, and you are not alone. We are with you. We know this is so hard for you. We know you want to keep your baby. We know you are just a child having a child. Even though it feels like you have no choice, you are choosing real love by giving your baby to Jesus.

You are loving this child like a real mother and giving her up for her sake. Even though you tried to stop the adoption, you still did what you thought was best for your baby. This baby will always be of your flesh and connected to you for all eternity. That was God's gift to you. You will not be punished for anything. You're not a bad person. All you ever wanted was to be loved and accepted.

Don't feel like a victim anymore. You are a child of God. God loves you. He wants to love you just as you are and be there for you, and release you from any guilt you have concerning everything. He loves you just the way you are.

Don't believe the lies of Satan any longer. God has not abandoned you and never will. He wants to fill the hole in your heart that was put there the day your baby was taken away from you. Jesus is all you need. Feel his loving arms around you. Feel his Sacred Heart inside of you. He loves you, and I love you, too.

— Cindy

Great letter, Cindy!

It moved me to tears. Why not take teenage Cindy out of the hospital room and go do something fun? Maybe you can go to a park, the mountains or the zoo. Ask her where she would like to go, and in your imagination go there with her.

Continue to read your letter over and over again. Create a conversation with her. Bring up any outstanding concerns that she may have and address them with love.

Afterwards, please share my letter with her:

Dear teenage Cindy,

Your parents are not your gods. You are *not* to live your life according to your parent's expectations. Your life belongs to the Lord. Jesus bought your life with his blood. He paid the price for your life on the cross. You belong to him and to no other. He loves you and has an incredible purpose and plan for your life.

Stop shaming yourself. Stop allowing your parents to shame

you. Shame and the sin of other people's expectations are like dirty filth on the beautiful recesses of your heart. You are the temple of the Holy Spirit. You belong to the Lord, and he is a jealous God. You are not to allow the false gods of shame and other people's expectations into your inner sanctuary. Your inner sanctuary is to remain clean and pure. The Lord loves you and wants you to be holy, as he is holy.

After you drive out the filthy intruder of other people's shame and expectations, I want you to invite the Lord Jesus into your heart to take its place. Ask Jesus to fill you, to comfort you, to nourish you, to restore you, to love you and to heal you. Will you please do that for him?

— Rob

Dear Rob,

I have been reading our letters to teenage Cindy. Every time, I let go of a little more darkness and let in a little more light. I have made a decision not to live in the shame of other people's expectations anymore, ever again. That no one, not even my parents, have the right to do that to me.

I have lived every minute of my life pleasing people. When I feel like I have failed in somebody's eyes, or God forbid, they get mad at me, or I felt rejected in some way, I'm always crushed beyond repair. I then turn to potato chips and ice cream to ease the pain.

My new concept has been, *I'm not guilty!* That's what you have helped me to see and accept from Jesus. This is huge, huger than you can imagine. I'm already feeling like I don't have to turn to food, or anything or anybody but Jesus. I feel the desire to turn to him more.

I'm still feeling lots of pain, but that's the key — feeling. Before I was trying to numb myself. For the first time in my life, I don't want to live numb anymore. It hurts worse to live life numb. It's not living anyway; it's dying a slow and heartless death.

This is a miracle to me. It's really working. Now I'm crying again, because you just can't imagine what it's been like living with all this guilt. I know this is just the beginning of the healing process, but already my heart is getting lighter. You were right about everything! I could never thank you enough if I started now and said it over and over for a million years. Where do we go from here?

— Love, Cindy

Dear Cindy,

How does teenage Cindy feel about the hospital scene? Is she feeling safe? Does she feel loved and supported? Is there any negativity left that we should work through before moving on to a different scene? Did you ever write your parents' apology letter? Your parents need to apologize to teenage Cindy — 100 loving words that she deserves to hear. *Dear Cindy, we are sorry for...*

When this scene is complete and teenage Cindy feels completely loved, send me the second worst event that has ever happened to you. We'll work through that situation next.

— Rob

Dear Rob,

Here's the letter from my parents:

Dearest daughter Cindy,

We're sorry for not letting you stay at home and for not supporting you through your pregnancy. We know you must have felt completely alone, scared and frightened. Out of our own hurt and fear, we sent you away. We should have kept you at home. We're sorry for never loving you the way you needed to be loved.

— Mom and Dad

I still have a lot of pain with the hospital scene and the baby's birth. I feel better walking with you and Jesus, but I still have a lot of guilt for getting pregnant in the first place, and for living the life I was living, and for giving my baby away afterwards. What kind of mother gives her baby away? Not to mention, I can't seem to let go of how scared I was the day of her birth.

I'm trying to see Jesus in the scene with me, but I physically start shaking just thinking of it. To this day, I live in *scare mode* all the time, waiting for the other shoe to drop. You're right, I'm not ready to move on. I will keep working on the hospital scene.

— Cindy

Dear Cindy,

My first thought is that you are taking on too much in one healing session. It will be helpful to work on one event at one time. We started working with teenage Cindy in the hospital, and now you're feeling terrible for getting pregnant in the first place and living in sin a year before the pregnancy. Stop! Finish the hospital scene. Find a way to bring it to completion.

After the hospital scene is complete and teenage Cindy is feeling loved and cared about, then surrender the day to the Lord in prayer and leave it in the past. Finished! Forgiven! Forever!

Once you are ready, move onto a different scene. I see three more scenes you will need to work through: getting pregnant, which probably happened nine months before the hospital scene; your lifestyle before getting pregnant; and signing the adoption papers.

Turn your healing process over to the Lord. Seek him in prayer and find out what he wants you to do next. Let me know what he says, and I will help you. If the Lord wants you to start a new scene that deals with the adoption papers, then send it over with all the details and we will work through it together.

— Rob

Dear Rob,

I think I'm OK with almost everything now, except for the signing of the papers. I can't get past the feeling that I'm going to die. It's the most intense pain I have ever felt in my heart. I can give my baby to Jesus in the white church, because I love him and trust him, but I signed away my baby to an attorney.

Looking back, it's hard to believe that after one signature, which only took two seconds, my baby was gone. I'm really having a hard time with this part. I think that's why I always feel guilty about everything, and always have a fear of rejection and loss. It's probably why I always try to please everybody.

The second hardest thing happened when I was 15. I tried to kill myself. My parents put me in a mental institution, where a lot of abuse happened. I'm scared to tell you all the stuff. Even saying this makes me feel like you'll think I'm a terrible person.

— Cindy

Dear Rob,

I'm trying to work on the memories, but I feel like I'm going to die if I keep eating like this. I don't know how to stop. Any help you could give me would really be appreciated. I need to stop it dead in its tracks. I can't go on like this any longer. I need to stop. Do you have any suggestions? I'm desperate, and you're the only one I know to turn to.

— Cindy

Dear Cindy,

I'm sorry for not getting back to you sooner. I just got back from an eight-day Texas tour. It was a powerful trip, and many people experienced profound healings from the Lord.

I fasted four days on juice and water before leaving, and I fasted six days and nights during my time there.

Fasting is converting food hunger into God hunger. Jesus fasted 40 days, Moses fasted 40 days, and Elijah fasted 40 days. How about a ten-day fast on vegetables and water? Please consider removing all the temptation from your house. Dedicate the next ten days to the Lord and fill your refrigerator with every kind of vegetable. Drink only water and eat as much cooked or raw vegetables as you like.

When you find your body craving breads and sugars, have some more vegetables and convert your food hunger into God hunger. Cry out to God, and he will fill you with his powerful presence.

— Rob

Dear Rob,

I have been spending time with you and the Lord in the hospital room. Somehow having you there gives me the confidence to move through the process. Jesus and I have spent time in the room, we signed the paper together. He held the paperwork instead of the attorney.

I really feel like I'm OK with the hospital scene. I never thought I would be able to say that, but I do. I really do. Thank you!

— Cindy

Chapter Five

Dear Cindy,

Good job cleaning up the hospital scene!

What are your thoughts on fasting? Are you ready to encounter God as never before? Are you ready for more healing work?

Pray about the next step in your journey — fasting or healing. Healing involves a lot of crying over past wounds. Fasting involves a lot of crying out to God to feed you supernaturally. When you are ready to heal another part of your past, send it over. Dig up all the pain, the hurt emotions, the hurtful words spoken and the sick things the doctors did to you.

Maybe you can get your family to join you on the vegetable fast and remove all other temptations from your house. It's only for a few days. I guarantee you it will be the most powerful time of your life.

We serve a wild God, and he desires to take you on a wild, passionate adventure. Surrender to him and be obedient. He will never let you down!

— Rob

Dear Rob,

Yes, I'm ready! I don't want to waste one more second not being closer to God. My heart has been burning to know him deeper.

I went to Adoration, confession, and Mass today. I went to see if my next step was the fasting. I have never been good at fasting. When I read your suggestion, my first thought was to tell you all kinds of reasons why I couldn't do it. I still don't think I can. I'm addicted to food — hello! Yet I had the feeling that I'm supposed to do it.

At first I decided to eat only vegetables, but not do the water. I thought the vegetables would be hard enough, but during Mass, my heart didn't want to hold anything back from God. I wanted to give him everything! I'm going to fast on vegetables and water. I hope you are praying! I've never been able to do anything like this before. More than anything, I want to get closer to God!

— Cindy

Excellent, Cindy!

Your response brought me great joy. Fasting is extremely powerful. Remember, fasting is not a diet. You are not denying yourself anything. Your motivation needs to be for God and God alone. You are converting food hunger into God hunger. Your spirit-woman needs to cry out to God. You need to feel your hunger for God and spend all your extra time in prayer and praise.

Allow God's spirit to feed you supernaturally. I will pray for you all week, every day, probably several times a day. Will your family support you? Will they fast with you? Can you remove all temptations from your house? When will you begin the fast?

— Rob

P.S. You may want to read the book of Daniel the first day of your fast.

Dear Rob,

I started fasting this morning. My family isn't going to join me, but that's OK. I couldn't get to church until noon, and that's when I ran it by the Lord.

I understand this is not a diet, but for someone who is addicted to food, this is very hard. It's even harder giving up coffee and tea. It's even harder doing it this week, because we are still in the process of moving.

I used to never miss daily Mass, but over the last couple years I have drifted away. I'm going to start back again every day. I have missed it. My soul has missed it. I don't know how it happened except that I would miss one here and there, for this reason and that. Two years later, I find myself struggling to make Mass on Sunday.

I can't tell you how hard the vegetables and water is for me. I'm not saying that to complain, but so that you understand. Being a food addict, which by the way is so painful to admit, has turned food and drink into a false god for me. And going from bingeing to just vegetables and water … I'm not feeling so good.

— Cindy

Dear Cindy,

It looks like the power of fasting has already started to change you. A month ago, you had no desire to attend daily Mass. Now your spirit-woman has a new longing.

Do you see the power in fasting? It transcends intellectual knowledge. In your mind you know daily Mass is good, but you can have all the intellectual knowledge in the world and your spirit-woman can still be dead and defeated by excuses.

Fasting has the power to take you from level 4 spirituality to level 7. It doesn't matter where you are in your walk with the Lord. If you are level 20, it will take you to level 25. Fasting is the most powerful way I know of to hear from God. It is the only guaranteed way I know of to hear from God. God honors fasting! God loves you so much that when you give up food for his sake, in exchange for his Presence, he will feed you supernaturally.

How are you fighting the temptations? Is your family supporting you? Encouraging you? Praying for you? Or are they trying to make you stumble? Are you using your warfare prayers when the temptations strike? Are you getting angry at evil for seducing you with a false god all these years? Are you angry at evil for all the harm it has caused you through this addiction?

Let's work on the temptations. Where are they coming from? Ask the Lord to show you. Are they coming from your family, your feelings or from the devil? I want to know the source. Let's remove the temptations today, so tomorrow you will be forever free.

— Rob

Dear Rob,

To even think about being free seems like a miracle to me. I have thought and prayed about this all day. I never saw food as a temptation, because I thought you had a choice in temptations, and it never feels as though I have a choice with food.

Something will come over me, and I will feel that I have to eat or drink a certain thing, or I will explode. I get filled with anxiety and guilt, and I'll eat and watch TV to zone out and avoid facing the pain of shame, rejection and my low self-esteem.

Sometimes my family will trigger these feelings. Sometimes it's situations. I feel I have no control in my life. If I don't do what other people want and they get mad at me, that makes me eat even more.

My family does not support my fasting, but to be fair, they don't understand the spiritual benefits. They don't understand a lot of things about me. I'm constantly trying to stay in all their good graces, just like when I lived with my parents.

What are the warfare prayers that I should be using to fight temptation? I think that's my worst problem. I've never known how to fight. I've always just given in, because I thought I had no choice. I now realize that has been an excuse for me. How do I fight? I'm angry at what evil has done to me!

— Cindy

P.S. Can the devil read your thoughts? I've always wanted to know.

Dear Cindy,

Let's start by taking a closer look at the statement you made in your last letter: "Something will come over me, and I will feel like I have to eat or drink a certain thing, or I will explode."

There are only three forces that can come over you and make you want to eat something. It's safe to assume that this force is not coming from the Lord. God doesn't force anyone to eat food, especially until you feel like exploding. If you want to stop eating and lose weight, but can't because you are constantly being driven by something, it is safe to assume this force is not coming from you. That only leaves one other possibility — evil.

The presence of evil in the world comes from fallen angels. Revelation 12 describes how God stripped these fallen angels of their power and kicked them out of heaven. The Bible says these spiritual entities prowl around like a roaring lion, looking for someone to devour. These fallen angels are called demons, and they can disguise themselves in many ways.

Ephesians 6:12 says, *For our struggle is not against enemies of blood and flesh, but against the rulers, against the authorities, against the cosmic powers of this present darkness, against the spiritual forces of evil in the heavenly places.* The force that comes over you is the presence of darkness. It can't hurt you unless you make agreements with it. It can only make you feel bad and whisper seductive temptations in your mind.

To fight this force, you need to get mad at it and say with your spirit-woman, *I bind you Satan in the name of Jesus and cast you into the lake of fire!* Keep repeating this over and over, a thousand times if necessary. Keep saying it until the temptation resides. You can also remind Satan that his time is short and his place is in the lake of fire. You can also paraphrase the quote from 1 John 4:4, *Greater is he who is in me than he who is in the world.*

When I asked if your family was supporting you, I found myself getting mad at them before I heard your answer. When a homeless man wants to stop drinking, guess who offers him the first drink? His closest so-called friends. Evil will try to pounce on you any way it can, especially through the people who are closest to you. Evil has been assigned to everyone, including your family members. You need to stand strong and learn to fight because your family needs you.

You can win this battle with the Word of God. If your family doesn't understand the spiritual benefits, maybe you can help them by explaining things. All you need to do is ask your family to support your efforts and explain the biblical reasons behind your fast. By explaining yourself, you will be teaching your family about God and showing them the way to holiness. If you are too afraid to help your family understand God, how can you expect God to use you to help other people? If you are unwilling to help your family learn about God, then who else will help them learn about God?

I'm not sure if the devil can read our thoughts. It doesn't matter. The devil's time is short, and his place is in the lake of fire. All you need to worry about is the devil's ability to insert thoughts into your mind. These thoughts sound like our own thoughts. You have the power to take control over your thoughts. When an evil thought enters your mind, cast it out. Philippians 4:8 tells us what we should be thinking about:

Finally, beloved, whatever is true, whatever is honorable, whatever is just, whatever is pure, whatever is pleasing, whatever is commendable, if there is any excellence and if there is anything worthy of praise, think about these things.

I'm glad you're starting to get angry! Get very angry and convert that anger into power, the power to make changes, the power to take action, the power to speak out, the power to take authority, the power to stand your ground and fight. Let me know what happens next.

— Rob

Dear Rob,

I told my family what I was doing and why. They are now supporting me as far as not saying anything negative, but I'm not doing well, physically. I have a lot of medical issues. I don't know if this is part of the problem, but I have been up most of the night praying for God's direction.

I can hardly function. I think I could continue if I added a little fruit and tea. Would that ruin anything? I'm not asking because I want it for me. I'm just trying to think of a way to be able to function.

Please don't be mad. I really want your help and guidance. My spiritual director used to tell me to be honest about everything and we would deal with it as it comes. I hope you know that with all my heart I want to be rid of this food addiction and any false gods in my life. I truly want to be closer to the Lord and to serve him, and to help my family, too.

I have rewritten this letter several times. I can hardly think. I don't want to walk away from a golden opportunity, but I have to be able to function. I'm just trying to be as honest with you the best I can. If you say I need to stay on the vegetables and water, then that is what I will do.

— Cindy

Dear Cindy,

The second day of the fast is the hardest. On the first and second days my blood sugar level drops. I'm cranky, cold, and my body throws a fit.

On the third day of the fast, my body chemistry changes. My body kicks into overdrive, and from the third day forward, I'm on a spiritual high. Something always happens on the third day. The third day forward is where fasting pays off. I realize the first two days are the hardest.

I drink decaf tea on my fast, with honey. It won't hurt anything. Go ahead and have some tea. God honors your efforts. I want you to cry out to God and be strong enough to listen to God, not to be in so much pain that you can't function.

Now I'm worried about you. Please tell me what's going on.

— Rob

Chapter Six

Dear Rob,

I should have checked my e-mail sooner! I will add the decaf tea. I'm having horrible headaches, weakness and muscle spasms. I didn't want to say anything, because I didn't want you to think I wanted a false god more than the Lord.

I really do think the spell Satan had on me with food has been broken. I have no desire to eat anything, anymore. I couldn't care less if I never ate again, except that I don't feel good. I couldn't even go to Mass this morning, and I really wanted to. I have been crying out to God to reveal the root issues of all my stuff, but so far I haven't heard anything.

— Cindy

Good job, Cindy!

You are suffering abuse and continue to stand strong!

I forgot to tell you the best part about fasting. When you fast, God moves, and when God moves, the work he does, is permanent. God doesn't do faulty or temporary work. When God works a miracle in you, it lasts forever.

Your last letter gave me great hope. Can you imagine if the spell Satan had on you with food has been permanently broken? That would make every second of the hard times you have endured these past few days priceless. You fast a week, and in return, God delivers you for a lifetime. We sure do serve a great God.

— Rob

Dear Rob,

Don't be worried. I'm going to give it at least another day to see if it gets better tomorrow. I want to do this. If it doesn't get better, I'll tell you.

— Cindy

Dear Cindy,

You may want to add salt to your diet, and vitamins. I think your body is throwing a fit from the caffeine withdrawal. It would be OK to have some V8 vegetable juice and salt. If you don't mind me asking, what have you been eating? I'm still worried about you.

— Rob

Dear Rob,

Don't be worried. It's getting better. I've been eating cherry tomatoes, canned corn, peas, raw lettuce, broccoli, and cauliflower. I'm really OK now. I know the Lord is working. I put some salt on my vegetables yesterday. I think it helped. I didn't even eat last night or this morning. I don't want to eat food. I just want to soak up spiritual food.

You were right about everything. This has closed the door on Satan and opened the door to the Holy Spirit. I would fast for a thousand weeks to reach this place. I have been trying to get here for years. Thank you! I will be offering my Mass for you this morning.

— Much love and gratitude, Cindy

Dear Cindy,

Please pray before breaking your fast. Does the Lord want you to break your fast by slowly returning to a healthy diet? Should you keep the fast going until we work through the mental ward abuse?

It sounds like you and Jesus are in a good place. It might be wise to stay there for as long as you can, or until you are released. The problem in breaking the fast is that once you leave that sweet place of intimacy with the Lord, it might be extremely hard to get back there the next time.

Once you break your fast, be careful not to start eating sweets. High sugar levels are very destructive to our bodies. Once you stop eating man-made sweets, your taste buds will adjust and fruit will become very sweet. Fruit is God's naturally sweet gift to you. God wants to bless you with all of his gifts, and man-made sweets will rob you of your ability to enjoy God's blessings.

— Rob

Dear Rob,

It's been hard at times, but I'm going to fast for at least six days, which will end Sunday morning. Do you think I should go longer? If we have to do the mental ward scene before I get off, let's get it over with. I've already started crying, and I haven't said anything yet. Just thinking about it brings up the hurt. You've got me to think about things I have buried for years.

I was 15 years old, living at home, in a verbally abusive situation my whole life. I couldn't take it anymore. I took a razor blade and cut my wrist about a hundred times. I still have the scars to this day. I guess I didn't cut deep enough, because I didn't die, and all it did was land me in a different kind of nightmare. They took me out of town again. Everything was always in another town, so that no one would know.

My father and my grandfather took me. I saw them both crying when they left. I begged them not to leave me there, but they did anyway. They took me into this big room filled with crazy people just like you see in the movies.

I was petrified. There were only three other teenagers, two boys and one girl, and we all became close friends immediately. I held on to them, because I was terrified. One of the boys named Mike became my boyfriend. The girl's name was Darlene. Everybody hated it there because we were locked in this room all day with all these crazy people. The nurses were in glass cages to protect themselves, and we were in the pit with everybody else.

I remember watching a movie in the gym once, but other than that, we were always in this big room with everybody all the time, unless we went in the bathroom. We used to go to the bathroom, just to escape.

One day, Darlene and I decided to hide in the mechanical room. For some reason nobody went down there. I don't even know how we got away from somebody to do it. Right away the sirens started going off, and they began looking for us. We stayed down there for hours. The room had large pipes and a hole in the floor. Before long, we were afraid water was going to come through the hole and we would drown, so we turned ourselves in.

They put us both in solitary confinement. They took off our clothes and wouldn't let us go to the bathroom or anything. No windows, nothing in the room. Once in a while I would see someone look through the tiny peephole. I now know why people yell in those places. It's not because you are crazy, it's because they drive you crazy.

I always said that if I ever got out alive, I would go back and do something about that place, so others wouldn't go through what I went through. I never did go back, nor do I want to. Solitary confinement lasted for about two days, I think. It was hard to know what time it was in there, but I think it got dark twice.

After they released me from solitary confinement, they separated us for a while, which was awful. Eventually, they let us into the room together again. That's when we figured out how to escape, although I can't remember now how we did it. I do remember it was freezing with snow on the ground, and we had to leave our shoes, socks and coats behind.

Once again the sirens went off. We ran and ran in the dark. We didn't know where we were going. We came to a highway, and this car stopped immediately. When it stopped, it was full of drunken guys.

I don't have a prejudiced bone in my body, but back then, black guys didn't like white girls. They forced liquor down us both, and raped Darlene. They were in the process of raping me when somehow I got away, and I ran down the road half naked.

After a policeman saw me on the side of the road and they caught the guys, the police took us to jail — us, not them, because we were runaways and the guys said we had been with them willingly. I don't know if the mental ward told my parents to come and get me, but they did after I spent the night in jail.

To this day, I can't watch shows where people are in jail. I was so afraid there, too. Nothing bad happened when I was in custody, except that the police didn't believe my story. My parents have never believed me either. A psychiatrist from the mental ward tried to have sex with me, and when I told them, they didn't believe me. As I'm writing all this, I'm wondering if you will believe me.

That's what happened. You have opened a very deep wound. I have never told this story to anybody. I really don't know why I'm telling this to you. I don't even know you. I'm feeling pretty scared right now. You won't do something bad to me, will you? I'm sorry I said that, but that's what I'm feeling. I have been sitting here crying and screaming as I'm writing this — horrible stuff from deep down.

The Lord just told me this is the source! It's so awful! Why did you make me remember? I should never have remembered! It's so terribly gut wrenchingly awful...

I'm sorry.

I just sent that last letter without reading it. I was crying out from the depth of my soul. I've been sitting here doing it for quite a while. Fortunately nobody is home. I think the Lord planned it that way. I'm sorry I said what I said, but you don't understand — this hurts so bad. I'm just typing words, and I have no way to cry out to you, like I'm crying out here.

Why did you make me remember? I never wanted to remember again. Now you probably think I'm crazy, too, just like everybody else. You will probably leave me, just like everybody else. I was almost raped twice — once as I told you, and once by a priest. That's another story, and I know I'm supposed to stay on one topic at a time.

I had to come back and start typing again, because I can't take the pain of just sitting here alone. I know the Lord's with me, but I still feel very frightened. I'm afraid my husband will come home, and how will I explain this to him? I'm sitting here crying so hard from such a deep place. It really seems worse than the hospital, and I didn't think anything could be worse than that.

I have a splitting headache now. This was a horrible thing to think about, and now I'm crying again. This headache is the worst. I should have done this in the day, because now I have a dark night ahead of me. The pain is so deep that I'm not sure anything matters anymore…

Chapter Seven

Dear Cindy,

I believe every word you said. I'm sorry that happened to you. I'm not going to leave you. I'm not going to hurt you. My only desire is to bring love and healing to teenage Cindy.

I'm very concerned about her. Right now she needs you. She needs someone to love her, to be with her, to tell her she has loving friends who are going to go back and visit her in that terrible place. We will stay with her. We will never leave her. We will never let her go.

Right now teenage Cindy needs big Cindy to go back and hold her. We will do healing work in the morning. Right now just go back and hold teenage Cindy. Love her, be with her, take the razor out of her hands and wrap her wrists in bandages. Tell her how special she is. Tell her how much you love her.

Just hold her and love her. Take her to a safe place. Take her into the light. Stay with her tonight. Don't let her go. Stay with her all night. I will write you in the morning. I will be with you in prayer tonight.

— Rob

Dear Rob,

I need to tell you about the priest thing, just to get it over with, because it's really hanging over me. I always feel like I'm going to go to hell for saying bad things about a priest. This was one area where my spiritual director failed me. I told it to him in confession about 50 times, but he told me to never talk about it after that, because you should never say bad things about a priest. This is exactly when I started gaining the weight. I was always super-thin before this happened.

I want to get this out of me. When I was a lot younger, I met a priest. He was handsome and charismatic. Everybody loved him, and everybody wanted to be in his presence. I truly believed, from the first time I met him, that he had special connections to God, although I really knew nothing about the Lord or the Catholic faith at that point.

After I met him, we became like brother and sister, even though there was a physical attraction. He was very sexual. I don't know any other way to say it. He talked about how women looked all the time. At that time I was attractive enough I guess, and I think he liked me, personally and the other way. He also liked me because he could control me. He would be so nice to me, and then he would berate me and bring me to my knees.

One night he was supposed to meet me at a convent, and afterwards, we were going to go out for dinner. He was giving a retreat at this convent the next day, and he left me waiting in front of the Blessed Sacrament for hours. When he came to pick me up, it was night and no one was left. The Blessed Sacrament was exposed, so he brought in a sister to take my place.

Father was staying at the convent, so he took me down the hall past all the nuns, saying hi to everybody as we went. I knew them, too, and they knew me. He took me into his room, and as soon as he shut the door, he gave me a big hug. This time the hug was different. Then he threw me on the bed. I started to scream, but he covered my mouth. He was very tall and very strong. I couldn't get away.

A part of me felt guilty, because part of me wanted him to love me. All the feelings were all mixed up inside of me. After I fought him for a while, he finally stopped. He got up, left me lying with half my clothes off, and said, "That was just a test. If you had sex with me, I would have known you were unfit for my ministry."

He just left me there and walked out. I heard him outside the room talking to the nuns who were outside in the living room.

I worked for this priest in his ministry for about two years. He never did anything like that again. I hope I don't go to hell for saying this, but I think I shook hands with the devil. He had me convinced he could bilocate and read minds. He used to be really nice to me, and then yell at me to make me cry, and then yell at me until I stopped. He would say bad stuff again, and then later, be so loving. It was a sick relationship. I thought he was getting his orders from God, and that he was some kind of prophet.

The last time I ever talked to him, he berated me on my birthday and told me I was unfit to be in his ministry. I forget why he got mad at me, but I was devastated. He had found another woman who took over his ministry, and I think she is still with him. I have never spoken to him since. He tried to get me to come back several times over a two-year period, although he never called me directly. He always had other people call me and tell me Father wanted me back. I never went back, only because my spiritual director (who died two years ago) told me never to go back.

I loved this priest, so I thought. I went to Medjugorje and the Holy Land with him. He taught me a lot about Mary, but he was also into alternative spirituality like Buddhism and Hinduism. He had a very strong will. He told a lot of stories about the Blessed Mother appearing to him, and a bunch of other unbelievable stories.

I also know he went after other women and girls. I take the blame for everything I did, but it was something I never got over, because he was a priest, and I will always hold them in a special place because they give us the Eucharist. I was always afraid Father put a spell on me or something, because he was like that.

We were out one night, and some drunk guys at the bar started coming towards us saying bad things to Father. He stared them down like you do a dog. They acted paralyzed and turned around and walked away. Stuff like that was always happening with him.

I'm really scared of him. He slept in our last house, and even slept in our bed. He blessed it, but I always wondered if he put a curse on it or something. He got so mad at me when I didn't come back to work for him. He told everybody I was in love with him, and he had to let me go.

I had to get all this out. I really don't want to tell you any of this, especially the priest part. I really don't want to send you this letter either, but I'm going to. If I'm going to go for the healing, I might as well go all the way. I have told you the worst now. I feel completely drained. I'm so scared because it's dark. I know Satan is going to use all this against me.

I don't want you to hate me. I'm afraid you are going to leave me. Why shouldn't you? You don't know me, and why are you spending all this time on a complete stranger? I really do feel bad I've taken up so much of your time already.

I don't know if God really did send you to help me, but I think he did, or I wouldn't be doing any of this. I have now told you my darkest secrets. I feel like I'm talking to you and God at the same time. I don't know how to heal any of this. I feel only darkness as I speak of it. I even sound crazy to myself. How could I have been so stupid and made so many mistakes? This is the source of my guilt, I just realized, everything that happened with Father.

Low self-esteem from my mother, shame from not being a better mother to my daughter, and guilt for what happened with Father. God just revealed all this to me as I'm writing this letter. I always thought all of it came from having a baby out of wedlock.

— Cindy

Dear Cindy,

You, Jesus and I need to go back in time. Our mission is to rescue teenage Cindy from the hands of sick doctors. Once again we are a powerful force, except this time Jesus is angry, extremely angry at the injustice that has occurred. Jesus has entrusted those doctors and nurses with special gifts to care for hurting people, and they have abused their professional responsibilities.

Jesus is armed with the whip of justice — the same whip he used to clean his Father's house. If one of those doctors smirks the wrong way, he will use the whip to clean the medical building. If you think kicking over the moneychanger's tables and letting all the animals go free was messy, just imagine what he will do to the freak-show doctor's office. I can see bottles of pills and papers flying all over.

I'm not too happy to hear what these quacks did to teenage Cindy either. I'm here to set her free, and I'm holding the Word of God in my hand. I want you to bring along some supplies for teenage Cindy. Bring a blanket in case she's cold in that room. Bring her clothes so that you can restore her dignity. Bring a backpack of supplies for her, a care package of whatever you think she needs. Put it all in a backpack and get ready to go.

I know Jesus is good to go, too. He's always ready to go. I have my Bible in hand, so whenever you are ready, let's kick down the doors and rescue teenage Cindy.

We proceed down the hall towards teenage Cindy's solitary confinement cell. If any of the doctors or nurses get in our way, I want you to put them in their place. I want you to assertively speak your mind. Tell them they are wrong! Tell them how they are hurting teenage Cindy. If they don't listen, order them to bow down and worship Jesus.

Allow me to open my Bible and read the Word of God. *As I live, says the Lord, every knee shall bow to me, and every tongue shall give praise to God.* All I need to do is speak the Word of God, and the doctor's bodies, which are brought to life by the Spirit of God, instantly obey.

After adult Cindy tells all the doctors and nurses how and why they are wrong, I want you to get the key from the doctor in charge, and then we will proceed to the solitary confinement cell. Unlock the door and help teenage Cindy get dressed. Turn on the light and wrap the blanket around her.

When she's ready to talk, I want you to listen to her. I want you to tell her she is *not* crazy. Tell her you love her. Tell her she doesn't belong here. Tell her that her parents were wrong to abandon her. Tell her that her parents were wrong to abuse her, neglect her and bring her to this place. Tell her the doctors and nurses are wrong because they have no love in their hearts.

Allow me to open the Bible and read a verse from 1 John 4: 7–8: *Let us love one another, because love is from God; everyone who loves is born of God and knows God. Whoever does not love does not know God, for God is love.* These doctors and nurses are wrong because they do not love and they do not know God. Without God and God's love there is no healing! Without God, all the doctors can do is lock hurting people up, dope them up on drugs, call God's children psychological names and write reports about their sufferings.

After you explain this to teenage Cindy, I want you to introduce teenage Cindy to the source of all love: Jesus. Allow her to pour out her heart to him. He is love itself. Jesus loves teenage Cindy. Jesus feels her pain. Allow teenage Cindy to fall into his arms. Allow Jesus' love to wash her clean. Allow Jesus' love to heal her and set her free.

After teenage Cindy accepts Jesus' love, forgiveness and healing, take her out of that place. Take her somewhere safe.

— With love, Rob

P.S. Thank you for sharing about the priest and the carload of punks. I'm looking forward to setting these perverts straight as well. But right now, I want you to stay with the solitary confinement scene until it's healed. I will be checking e-mail all day.

Dear Rob,

We went and got her. She's free, but she's frail like a puppy dog that's had her spirit broken. She is clothed and warm. I remember how cold she was. I felt her hands and they were ice cold. Her eyes were almost swollen shut with tears. They were filled with such fear. Jesus picked her up, took her out and told everybody she would never be back, and that she should never have been there in the first place.

He took her to his house, because she has always felt safe in church. This church was beautiful. There were lots of inspiring statues, a huge crucifix in white and lots of candles giving off warmth.

She finally quit shivering after Jesus sat her down in the pew. He never left her side. He still had his arm around her. You were on the other side of her. She was surrounded and protected. No one can ever hurt her here or take her back to that place again.

While we were there, Jesus took a baseball bat and broke the glass surrounding the nurse's station, so the staff couldn't sit in there and be untouched. He told them to help his people, or he would come back, and they would be sorry. I also asked him to help this one man who I felt so sorry for. I don't think I ever knew his name. He was more frightened than I was.

Jesus went over and touched him and healed him, too, but he never let go of me all the while. Teenage Cindy was so thin and frail. Jesus held her in his mighty arms with sweet gentleness, but firmness. You and I surrounded them as he carried her out.

* * * *

Now that we are in the church, there are sweet smelling flowers, and everything is bright and beautiful and warm. I know I will never have to go back to that institution ever again, and that Jesus will make sure they never hurt people like that again. That's comforting to me. I don't want others hurt either.

I love listening and watching you read to teenage Cindy in this vision. Your voice sounds like Saint Michael the Archangel, kind yet very strong. You speak for the Lord, and he nods approval as you read. Jesus is still holding teenage Cindy. He has his white cloak all around her. She can even smell his sweetness, and she can feel his heart beat with her head on his chest, like Saint John at the Last Supper.

Finally she is free from all doctors, which the Lord told her she never needed in the first place. She only needed to be loved. He told her he will never leave her or reject her, no matter what she does or doesn't do. She doesn't have to earn love anymore, or be afraid, because Jesus won't let anybody from that place ever hurt her again.

The Word of God is like a beautiful white fence around the church, protecting it from all evil. She knows in her heart, for the first time, that she is really safe. She now knows that she's not crazy. It's not crazy to want to be loved.

Teenage Cindy told Jesus everything. I told him I'm sorry for cutting my arm with the razor blade and that I will never do anything like that again. He looked in my eyes and forgave me for everything. He caressed my hair. His eyes are so comforting and filled with love.

I know he forgives me and will always be there to protect me. I hug his neck so tight. I don't feel alone anymore. I look over at you, and you are smiling, too. I'm glad you are also there, Rob. You told Jesus I was there, and that's why he came to get me. Thank you for telling Jesus so that he came for me.

— Cindy

Good work, Cindy!

Your letter made me cry. I know how hard you have worked all week. I would say you are cleared to break your fast Sunday morning, but you had better make sure it's OK with the Lord. I will leave that decision up to you and the Lord. If you're not hungry, you may consider keeping it going.

If you break the fast, I would like to ask you to keep the spirit of fasting going for another week. Just start incorporating healthy foods, along with the vegetables, into your diet. Another idea is to ask the Lord's permission and give him thanks and praise before you eat anything all week.

If you break the fast on Sunday, the first day of the week, the day Jesus set us free, I would take the day to celebrate Jesus and all the powerful work he has done in your life. Wow, what an incredible week. I would take a day of rest. Refresh your spirit-woman. Do something peaceful, restful and spiritually rewarding. Do you like getting out in nature?

— Rob

Chapter Eight

Dear Rob,

After Mass this morning when I went to break the fast, it felt like the Lord was giving me back coffee as a gift because I used to love it so much, but I think I'm going to give it up again. It doesn't taste as good as it used to, and a few times, I thought it was going to make me sick.

I'm going back to decaf tea. I didn't want to break my fast yet, and I'm not going to. I don't think the Lord wants me to either. I'm not taking a bite of anything until he tells me I can. I don't care if I never eat anything but vegetables the rest of my life, if that's his will for me.

Except for the coffee incident, this morning was wonderful, but I have been under terrible attack this afternoon. My mother called, and she hardly ever calls me. My calls with her are never good. It makes me sad that it has always been like this. Don't be worried, I'm not giving in. I still feel strong, but I don't know where this darkness is coming from or why. I'm just going to keep praying and singing songs of praise. No one is home but me, and I have the music up very loud!

— Cindy

Dear Cindy,

Do you remember how much pain you were in on the second day of the fast? I believe it was mostly caused by caffeine withdrawal. Your body was addicted to high sugar intake, caffeine, unhealthy chemicals and who knows what else.

On the second and third day your body threw a fit, and it almost killed you. Please do not go back to sugar, chemicals and caffeine. If God didn't put it on this earth naturally, please don't put it in your mouth.

Coffee doesn't taste good anymore because it is unhealthy for your body. God honored your fast and took you to a higher spiritual level. The fast also cleaned the unhealthy toxins out of your body. It broke your food, chemical and caffeine addictions.

If you go back to eating all the junk that you did before, your body will once again develop the same addictions. Please do not go back there ever again. If you do, you may not have as much of God's grace to get free. Keep in mind there are plenty of evil forces at work that would like to see you fall back into bondage.

Do you have any other food addiction questions? Are you ready to do more healing work? Let me know when you are ready, and I will spend time in front of the tabernacle and send over another imagination technique for you to work through.

— Rob

Dear Rob,

I know how addicted I was to Diet Coke and coffee, and I don't want to go down that road again either. I want no false gods before him. I have already put the coffee and filters back in the cupboard for company only. I'm not drinking it anymore. I really don't want to.

At first I thought the Lord was giving me coffee as a gift. Now I think he just wanted me to see the truth you are speaking. It will be harder to be rid of the Diet Coke. If you say I shouldn't drink or eat anything with chemicals, then I know that includes Diet Coke. I'm going right now to get rid of it. Are canned vegetables OK? That's what I've been living on.

In the past I used to drink. Any time a thought of any of this stuff came to mind, I would pour myself another shot. God broke me of that many years ago. I also used to smoke. He broke me of that, too. Now I'm ready to conquer this food addiction. It has been the longest and the hardest. I don't want to take any steps backwards. I hope I didn't mess anything up with the coffee.

I'm ready for more healing, if you don't mind. I don't want to take up too much of your time. I still can't believe I have gotten through the hospital and the mental ward and I still feel released. I never thought that could happen.

— Cindy

Dear Cindy,

Millions of Americans are addicted to caffeine. It's no different than any other mood-altering substance — it's a false high. We feel more energized after drinking a cup, but afterwards, our bodies have to work overtime to get rid of the chemicals. It robs us of our rest and pollutes our bodies with harmful toxins.

Have you ever peeled an apple and watched how fast it turns brown? It turns brown within minutes because the apple is alive and full of enzymes. As soon as it is cut, the air hits it and it starts to decompose. All fresh fruits and vegetables are alive. They contain vitamins, minerals and enzymes, all of which your body needs to be healthy.

Have you ever wondered why vitamins are in dark bottles? To keep the sunlight from killing the living nutrients. All canned food is dead. Almost all bottled fruit juice is dead. If the label says the product has been pasteurized, it means they ran it through a process to kill all the living bacteria, vitamins and enzymes.

Please try to eat as much fresh produce as possible. Fresh is always better than canned. Raw is better than cooked. Steamed is better than boiled. Give your body what it needs, and it will be less likely to crave what it doesn't need.

— Rob

Dear Rob,

OK, the Diet Coke is out of here! I was also drinking a regular tea when you e-mailed me, and that is down the drain, too. I hope I haven't messed anything up by already drinking coffee and regular tea a little bit. I'm back on water and decaf only.

I forgot to tell you, do you remember how cluttered my house was? Well, we have been moving into our new place, and guess what? I've been tossing junk like nobody's business. I don't need all this stuff anymore. I don't need any more self-help books either, because God is my healer.

The Lord has also freed me from an addiction to secular magazines. I would buy them all the time, and I never got a chance to read them. When I would read them, they would cause me all kinds of anxiety. I have been throwing away truck-loads, unread!

I don't ever want to go back to that place again. Do you think I'll remain strong?

— Cindy

Dear Cindy,

Yes, I think you will stand strong!

You will probably drop 60 pounds within the next six months. After that, I hope the Lord calls you into full-time ministry to help deliver other people who are suffering the same kind of pain. All you need to do is keep your eyes on the Lord and continue to take your healing process seriously.

At some point we will need to deal with the drunk guys who tried to rape you. I want you to ask the Lord to bring up all the painful emotions, memories and fears regarding this situation. Write them all down and send them over whenever you are ready.

— Rob

Dear Rob,

It's winter and so cold. They took our coats, shoes and socks, so if anyone did escape they couldn't get far. We didn't know where to run, but we just keep running, little Darlene and little Cindy. We're crying and running, because we know if we get caught, we will have to go back to solitary confinement.

We are both so cold! We can't stop shivering! We see lights, there's a road ahead, and we see a car. We run towards it yelling *stop, please stop*. They do. It's a car full of black guys. I get scared immediately, but Darlene says, "Come on, it will be OK. If we go back, they'll put us in solitary confinement, and you know how horrible that is!"

After approaching the car, Darlene walks up to the passenger side window and says, "We were on dates, and our dates got mad at us, and took our coats, socks and shoes. Will you please take us into town?"

The guy in the front seat says, "Sure, hop in."

Right away they start flirting and touching us, but not too badly at first. We go along with it a little bit, joking, not kissing or anything, just to get the ride. I didn't know how far it was to town, because we were out in the country.

Darlene was my protector, and she tries to talk them into taking us into town so we can change and go to a bar, but they are not going for it. They take out the booze and start pouring it down us. She has two guys fighting her in the backseat, but I'm in the front seat, and I just have one. The other guy is driving.

We're screaming, and they are saying all kinds of terrible

things and calling us names. I really think I hear Satan speaking. I'm trying to get the guys off Darlene. The guy in the front is trying to get the booze down me. The guys in the back have half Darlene's clothes off. I see her eyes, and I can't do anything. They start raping her, and I can't stop it!

Then the guy in front starts to take my clothes off. He just gets my shirt off, and for some reason, the car stops. I think the driver is going to join in. Somehow I get the door open and jump out, and I'm running down the road screaming, with my shirt off. One of the guys is chasing me. Then out of nowhere, a police car appears. I run up to it and scream, "Help me, they are raping my friend!"

The guys throw Darlene out of the car and take off. The police catch them later, but let them go. They take us to jail and lock us up when they find out we're runaways. My parents come and get me the next day, and I never get to see Darlene again. I felt so bad that I couldn't help her. I wanted to run away as bad as she did. It was my fault just as much as hers. I never got to tell her how sorry I was for what happened. Plus I loved her. We were all each other had for a long time. She was my protector in that place.

I couldn't do anything to save her. I can still see her eyes. I can still see their eyes. They were so cold and piercing. Why did we get in the car? I have been afraid of men ever since that happened. Not just sexually, but in all ways; afraid of their voices, their physical strength. I can still feel their hands all over me. It was such a terrible feeling.

— Cindy

Dear Cindy,

I want you to go back to the parked-car scene, but this time, take Jesus and me with you. As soon as I see a parked car with a bunch of guys raping two innocent girls, I run up to the door and immediately the window shatters. It must have been the Lord because I didn't touch it. I was going to open the car door and pull these guys out one by one, but since the window shattered and captured everyone's attention, I pull the first guy out though the window by his neck.

He's only a teenage punk kid, so it doesn't take much to hurl him through the air. The driver gets scared and tries to start the car to get away, but I pull the keys from the ignition and hand them to Jesus. The Lord doesn't say anything, but by the look on his face, he is extremely serious about putting an end to this injustice.

The driver comes out through the broken window, too. While I'm pulling him out by his neck, I want big Cindy to start praying deliverance prayers. Jesus has already given you the power. Have Jesus give you more power, and I want you to start binding up and having any demonic influence over this situation destroyed.

As you are praying, I open the door and grab the two guys in the backseat by their necks. As I'm pulling them out of the car, their heads accidentally crack together. A part of me wants to hurt them, but when I see how scared they are, instead of throwing them though the air, I walk them over and sit them down next to their buddies.

I'm going to stand guard over the boys until the police arrive. Until then, I want you to go with Jesus and comfort the girls. Jesus has some blankets and white robes to help warm the girls. I want you to tell them it is not their fault. I want big Cindy to love and comfort little Cindy and Darlene until they stop shaking.

Ask Jesus to take the cleansing fire of his Holy Spirit and burn off all the areas where these guys touched the girls. Have Jesus put his healing hands over any area of little Cindy's body where it still feels sick. Allow Jesus to speak loving words of healing and power into her life. Take as much time as necessary ministering to little Cindy and Darlene.

After little Cindy and Darlene are completely OK, I want big Cindy to stand next to me and confront the abusers. I want you to tell them how much they have hurt little Cindy and Darlene. Tell them how their sick behaviors have affected Cindy her entire life. Tell them little Cindy is a child of God and that no one is allowed to violate her purity. Tell them about the sanctity of human sexuality. Tell them about heaven and hell. Tell them if they don't bow down and ask Jesus for forgiveness they could be eternally separated from God.

If you see sorrow in their eyes, have them apologize to Jesus and allow Jesus to heal and forgive them of their sickness. If you see some sign of repentance, but they are still cold and evil-looking, keep talking to them. Tell them more about God's judgment and about God's merciful love. If there's no sign of repentance, have the police come and take them away.

Even if the guys repent and Jesus forgives their sins, the police still need to come and take them away. Jesus wants these kids arrested and their parents notified so that he can continue working in their lives.

After the police leave, I want big Cindy to minister to Darlene until the light of Christ is glowing in her eyes. If she doesn't know about Jesus, please introduce her to your friend. Allow Jesus' love to fill little Cindy's and Darlene's eyes until they are shining brightly with the love of Christ.

Afterwards, please allow Jesus to take the girls to a safe, beautiful place where they can be warm and free.

— With love, Rob

Chapter Nine

Dear Rob,

I spent the last four hours in Adoration, praying and forgiving everybody. I'm totally exhausted. I told them what they did to us was wrong, and I felt they were sorry. I kept telling little Cindy and little Darlene over and over that it wasn't their fault. It took a long time to calm them down. I also put the blankets and robes on them. They were so cold.

I asked the Holy Spirit to come and heal all parts of my body that had been touched and defiled. I could feel the Holy Spirit all through me. It was so wonderful. I kept telling Darlene how sorry I was that I couldn't save her, and we spent a lot of time talking. I know she forgives me, and doesn't blame me.

I told the guys how much they hurt little Cindy and little Darlene. I wanted to believe they were sorry. I didn't tell them about heaven, hell or God or anything, but I'm sure they were sorry. I tried to see them in my imagination, but I couldn't remember what they looked like. I can remember Darlene, but not them.

I feel so much better about everything, but what surprised me the most was how I cried. I have never cried like that before. I couldn't stop for an hour! It was so deep down and gut-wrenching. My body is still sore from it. Those were the most gut-wrenching primal tears I have ever shed in my entire life. It came out of me from such a deep place that I thought I was going to start vomiting.

I feel I'm in a state of shock. It was as though time stood still, especially for that hour or so, when the Lord took care of me. I can't believe you helped me do this.

— Thank you, a million times, Cindy

Good work, Cindy!

It sounds like you had a powerful healing experience.

I went to church last night to pray for guidance on the next step of your healing process, and I will need some more information from you in order to proceed. In one of your previous letters you say you went to confession at least 50 times in regards to the priest issue and still do not feel free from the situation. I believe this is good discernment. I need you to dig a little deeper. I know what I'm looking for, but I want you to discover it with the Lord's help.

In your letter you describe both emotional and sexual abuse with the so-called priest. Maybe we should refer to him as a cleric, because he doesn't deserve the title of priest. If the night in the convent was the worst event that has happened to you, we will need to start there. If there's another situation that hurt you more, I would like to hear about what else happened.

I need for you to go back to the convent room and dig a little deeper. What exactly happened? Are you holding anything back? I need to hear the full disclosure. Did this man take his clothes off? I need for you to go back there, dig up all the hurt and send it over. I'm standing by and will respond to you as soon as I hear the rest of the story.

— Rob

Dear Rob,

I'm not doing well at all, but don't be worried. I will fight through this. I have been trying to do what you said ever since I received your letter, and the battle is on. I can't get anything, and I'm getting more agitated and frightened.

I'm going to go downtown for Mass at noon. I'm feeling really scared. I want to be honest about everything, but I keep hearing this voice saying that I shouldn't tell you anything anymore. I'm sure it's from the dark side.

— Cindy

Dear Rob,

The feeling has come over me again. I don't believe it in my heart, but it's there, and I just thought I should tell you — the feeling that you are going to hurt me and leave me. That you are going to use this against me somehow.

Please don't leave me, Rob. I'm so scared. I can't do this yet. I'm going to have to go to Mass again. The next Mass isn't until evening. I've been sitting here trying to do this all day, and I can't. I'm so ashamed. I'm embarrassed about everything now.

— Cindy

Dear Cindy,

I asked you to go deeper for several reasons. When we are dealing with a gang of street kids who attack an innocent victim, then to heal that experience, I ask the victim to go back and dig up all the pain. Once the victim is in the midst of the pain, then it is possible to surrender the situation to the Lord, forgive the street gang and be set free.

Part of the reason I'm asking you to dig deeper is to bring up all the memories so that they are fresh. The other and more important reason is finding all the hooks and agreements that you have made with the enemy. Unlike the street gang scenario, with the cleric you are not an innocent victim. Directly and indirectly you opened yourself up to evil from this man.

This man has been involved in alternative types of spirituality, and the magnetic attraction that surrounds him and allows him to seduce women and stare down men at the bar, is *not* from the Holy Spirit. Through your sinful involvement and attraction to him you have opened yourself up to the demonic.

Do you think the demonic filth that has jumped onto you through this man *wants* you to uncover the source, the open door, the unconfessed sin and the hidden details that are allowing darkness access into your life? I believe you when you say, "The battle is on."

In this healing, we will need to do some spiritual warfare work. Let me know when you are ready. It may help you to reread the letter you sent a few days ago. I need you to dig up stuff that you may not be aware of, or may not think is important. For example, if a man tried to rape you, why did you continue to work for him two more years? What kept you under his spell? I'm sorry for the bluntness of this question, but did you ever perform sexual favors for him?

— Rob

Dear Rob,

I just put my husband on a plane for a couple days. This will be a good time for me to do this, so I can be alone with the Lord and cry as needed. It's hard for me to let go if I know someone might walk in on me and I would have to explain why I was crying. I don't think it's by accident that the Lord put me alone this day.

I didn't enjoy the question you asked, but I'm not offended. No, I did *not* perform any sexual favors for the cleric. I did want him to love me, but not sexually. I never wanted that. I did a lot of things that were wrong, but I think I'm going to have to give you this as it comes. The whole thing is coming in bits and pieces.

I would say that night was the worst, but it was only one of many things. He was and still is very involved in alternative spirituality. I can't remember what he called it, but he talked about it a lot. He also has a fixation with numbers.

Before I go back to that night, I want to tell you other stuff. I did want him to hold and hug me. Did I want him to love me? Yes. I really did not want him to have sex with me — although on some level, I think I did. I dressed for him. He used to constantly talk about other women, and I would do anything to please him. I would have done anything for him. I loved him. A part of me still does. How sick does that make me? Mostly, I'm just afraid of him.

I know he puts spells on other people. I suppose he might have put one on me, especially after he got mad at me. He used to tell me all kinds of things. He told me one woman committed suicide over him because he left her. What is wrong with me that I stayed with a man like that? At the time he convinced me that he was special and that women were attracted to him. He said he couldn't help it.

The night he tried to have sex with me, he told me he had sex with other women, but if they gave in to him, then he left them right then and there. He said that if I had said yes, he would have known I was not pure enough to run his ministry.

You have to understand I was in a different place then. I was extremely gullible. I used to believe anything anybody told me; especially a priest.

When I was in Medjugorje with him, about 14 of us saw the Blessed Mother. He said he allowed us to see her because he asked her to. Now I don't know if we actually saw the Blessed Mother, or an Angel of Light he conjured up. Maybe she did allow us to see her, and it had nothing to do with him. I don't know anymore. I had so many experiences like that with him. I think he originally chose me because he knew he could control my mind.

I look back now and see it as brainwashing — the kindness and then the berating, and then the kindness again. Why would I want to be with someone like that? At the time I thought he was doing the Lord's work, and I thought I was, too.

No, I'm not innocent in this, far from it. My computer is acting up again. I'm going to send this on, before I lose it, and then write some more…

OK Rob,

I think I did want to have sex with him. Are you happy? I said it. I suppose that is what you and the Lord are looking for. I wanted to have sex with a priest. I loved him. I loved him because somehow, in my twisted mind, I thought he was close to God. I had never cheated on my husband in 30 years of marriage, and I'm not going to choose a priest to do it with.

OK, you've got me where you want me. I feel like the scum of the earth. Not only would it be a sin of adultery, but a sacrilege. It's true that he forced himself on me, and when push came to shove, I couldn't do it. I remember crying out to God, "Help me. Please stop him from doing this." I was so scared. I didn't think I was going to be able to stop him.

I tried to stop him, and I couldn't. I just kept begging him, "Father, please stop. This isn't right. Please stop." I begged him for a long time before he would stop. He never got all his clothes off. I remember him taking off his belt with one hand, and unzipping his pants, and holding me down with the other, but that's as far as he got. I kept saying over and over, "Father stop. Please stop. This isn't right."

That's when he told me that if I had given in, I would have been unfit to run his ministry. He said other women had given in to him, and the next morning he left them because they weren't fit. He admitted to having sex with other women, and that should have been enough right there to show me he wasn't of the Lord; but somehow he convinced me it was a test. Now, I don't know why I believed him.

Like I said, I would have done anything for him. People to this day are still like that around him. He has this spell over people. Yes, I did love him, and I wanted him to love me back. On most levels, I felt like we were brother and sister — really close. I loved being loved by a priest. I have always been close to priests and nuns. It was especially wonderful to be loved by a priest I thought was a prophet.

The sex thing never came up again. Yes, I still dressed to please him. He wanted me to, and he demanded it. He ran a tight ship, and I wanted to please him and dress for him. I wanted his attention. I wanted his love. I would have done anything for him. When other women called to tell me he had made advances or something, I stood up for him.

Even though he had done this to me, the reality of it was clouded in my mind. I stood up for him and said he would never do anything like that. Instead of helping these poor women, I stood up for him.

I still think he put a spell on me. My spiritual director did exorcisms on me. Maybe they didn't take because I didn't confess my sin in the whole thing. He didn't want me to talk about it, because he said you should never criticize a priest.

I think the cleric put a curse on me when he got mad at me, and I think he put a curse on my house. Maybe I did it to myself because I opened myself up to the dark world, like you said, through this cleric. I don't know. I'm really scared now — really scared. I'm scared of Satan, and I'm scared to tell you all this.

It's been many years since I've talked to him. The last day was on my birthday. He yelled at me for literally 30 minutes and told me I was not worthy to run his ministry anymore. He found someone else to take over. In fact, she was a close friend of mine. To this day, she doesn't know why I will not come back. I heard her husband tried to commit suicide. Two days later, she left with Father to go to the Holy Land with him. When I heard that, I felt sick.

I'm feeling pretty dark as I'm writing this to you. Lots of memories are starting to come back, and they're not good. He was always so good at explaining everything away. For the first time, I'm starting to see things as they really were.

— Cindy

Chapter Ten

Good job, Cindy!

It's time to get free from this man's sickness! I want to start with another imagination technique. Let's go back and set young Cindy free.

You, Jesus and I go back in time. Jesus is extremely serious. I have never seen him so serious. I want you to picture us walking down the hallway. The three of us are standing outside the door listening to young Cindy's muffled screams. The cleric has taken off his belt. He wants to have sex with the young woman but she continues to fight him. Young Cindy is calling out for help.

Are you ready to burst through the door and help her? Or should we stand outside the room and pretend we are imagining things? She needs your help! Are you going to help her, or should we make excuses and try to explain things away?

When you are ready, Jesus wants you to open the door, shove the pervert off young Cindy and rescue her from his sickness. I want you and Jesus to take her back to the chapel and have a talk with her. Tell her Jesus has heard her cry for help and you are here with him to set her free. Meanwhile, I will stay behind with the cleric because we are going to have a little Bible study.

Once you are inside the chapel with Jesus, I want adult Cindy to love her. Tell her it's not her fault. Tell her it's OK to want to be loved by others. There is no sin in wanting to be loved. God created her with the desire to love and to be loved.

I want you to warn young Cindy about how dangerous this man is. She doesn't know about the evil forces in alternative forms of spirituality, and she is in great danger. Please warn her. It's not her fault for not knowing any better. The Lord will not hold her accountable for what she doesn't know.

After you have explained the dangers to young Cindy, I want you to help her confess her sins to Jesus. Tell her it's a sin to dress and act sexy. Tell her the sin of dressing that way can lead to scandal, especially if it causes men to lust or covet. Tell her the desire to have sex with anyone outside the confines of a God-approved marriage is a sin. Tell her it is a sin to covet someone sexually who has made vows of lifetime celibacy.

I know how sorry she is, and so does Jesus. Please help young Cindy to confess the sin of lying. She needs to confess the sin of standing up for evil and making excuses for the cleric's inappropriate behaviors. When young Cindy refused to stand up for the truth, she took sides with the devil. When she allowed the cleric's evil actions to continue, she committed a sin against the innocent women who were crying out to her for help.

I know how sorry she is, and so does Jesus. After she sees

the wrong she has done, ask the Lord if there's anything else she needs to confess. If there's nothing else to confess, allow her to be reunited with Jesus. Allow her to fall into his arms. Allow her to receive his love. Allow her to be washed clean and completely forgiven.

— Rob

Dear Rob,

I don't deserve to be forgiven. No wonder I always thought Jesus couldn't love me. How could he? I'm not sure I'm going to live through this night. It hurts so bad. I'm so sorry for everything — all the sins of my whole life.

— Cindy

Dear Cindy,

After you work through the forgiveness process, I want you and young Cindy to go back to the cleric's room. Don't worry; it's safe. I have him tied up with a rope. We are studying Matthew 7:15, *Beware of false prophets, who come to you in sheep's clothing but inwardly are ravenous wolves.*

After you walk into the room, I want you to hear every word that I'm speaking to the cleric: "According to this scripture passage, it sounds like you are a ravenous wolf who seduces women and that you are filled with every kind of spiritual sickness. That makes your sin ten times worse. If you were just an average pervert, your punishment would be severe, but because you dress up like a priest and abuse God's children, your punishment will be a thousand times greater.

"Luke 17:2 says, *It would be better for you if a millstone were hung around your neck and you were thrown into the sea than for you to cause one of these little ones to stumble.*

"Not only have you caused many little ones to stumble with your sick philosophy, but you have taken advantage of young Cindy. You screwed with her mind, polluted her thoughts, abused her emotionally, and if all that is not bad enough, you tried to have sex with her.

"2 Peter 2: 1–3 warns us about men like you: *False prophets also arose among the people, just as there will be false teachers among you, who will secretly bring in destructive opinions. They will even deny the Master who bought them – bringing swift destruction on themselves. Even so, many will follow their licentious ways, and because of these teachers the way of truth will be maligned. And in their greed they will exploit you with deceptive words. Their condemnation, pronounced against them long ago, has not been idle, and their destruction is not asleep.*

"It sounds like you are a false prophet. You are not teaching the Gospel of Jesus Christ. You have maligned the way of the truth. You have brought in your own demon-infested theology.

"Matthew 3:10 says, *Even now the ax is lying at the root of the trees; every tree therefore that does not bear good fruit is cut down and thrown into the fire.*"

After listening to all this, I want adult Cindy and young Cindy to tell him why it's wrong for a man to lust after a woman. Tell him why it's wrong to make his staff dress in seductive clothing.

Please tell him the standards of our Lord as defined in Matthew 5:29: *If your right eye causes you to sin, tear it out and throw it away; it is better for you to lose one of your members than for your whole body to be thrown into hell.*

Feel free to tell the cleric anything else you need to tell him. Tell him you send back all his sickness. Tell him you send back all his curses to be replaced with the gift of the Holy Spirit's conviction. Send back all his sickness and denounce everything that has to do with him. Tell him it was wrong to lie and make excuses every time he tried to rape, molest or make sexual advances towards women in his so-called ministry.

Tell him you regret working for him. Tell him you regret having him stay in your house. Tell him you regret promoting his spirituality within the Catholic Church. Tell him that unless he repents and changes his ways, he runs the risk of eternal separation from God. After you get through denouncing everything, ask the Lord what he wants you to do next.

— Rob

Dear Rob,

I have read both letters many times and cried about a thousand tears. I keep thinking that I'm the sinner. Am I going to be responsible for him going to hell? What about all the women whom I failed? Will I go to hell for those souls, too?

Part of me was eating myself to death because I knew the cleric would never have anything to do with a fat person. The other part of me was eating myself to death to punish myself. I always knew that I deserve to be punished. I don't feel I have the right to call on the Lord's name anymore.

I can't figure out a way to forgive myself for all this. Do I need to go to confession again? I don't want to go to hell. I can't accept Jesus' forgiveness, because I deserve to go to hell.

— Cindy

Dear Rob,

I don't feel like I will ever be close to God again. I have always been the queen of guilt, but this time the guilt is really justified. How do I get past it? I went from a thousand to a millions tears last night. Maybe I have to go to a billion. I just feel that God could never love me now, and I don't feel I can call Jesus Lord anymore.

I think this is what purgatory must feel like. It's a really bad place to be — not to be able to feel the love of God. I wouldn't do anything to hurt myself, but not feeling God's presence is worse than death…

Dear Rob,

I went to confession after Mass. The priest told me to let go of my guilt by asking Jesus to help put it all behind me. He said, "It's all forgiven now, just keep walking away from it, and keep going."

"How do you do that?" I said.

"It's not easy," he said. "Take it one day at a time and just keep asking Jesus to help you."

I can't ask for what I don't deserve! I feel so unworthy even though I have been praying for the cleric. I don't want him to go to hell either.

I tried my best to confess it all — my lust for the priest, my dressing for him, staying with a man who was involved in evil and for not helping the poor women who came to me. Do you think I got it all?

— Cindy

I'm sorry, Cindy.

I shouldn't have sent the second healing letter until you finished working through the first one. You need to work through the forgiveness scene in the chapel with young Cindy and finish it, before moving on. There are no magic quick fixes here. If you want to be healed from the experience, you will need to get into your heart and do your healing work.

Going to confession may help a little, but you can go to confession 50 times and still never reach a complete act of contrition. I'm not thinking 53 times is the magic confession number, either. I'm asking you to take this very seriously, get into your heart, and work through the scene. Don't stop until you have accepted the Lord's love and forgiveness!

You also need to forget about hell right now. If you reread the first letter, you will find no mention of hell anywhere.

— Rob

Dear Rob,

Something came over me last night, and I started feeling worse than before. All of a sudden this impenetrable darkness came crashing down. I couldn't get rid of it. I'm sure this is the spiritual warfare you've been talking about.

I never ate a bite of food all day yesterday. I didn't eat today either, until just a minute ago, and I'm still just eating vegetables and water. I'm not giving up. I'm sorry I got so pathetic on you the last few days. I was feeling that way, but I should have fought back.

I want to get this over with, and I sure don't want anything to do with this cleric ever again. I hope you know that. I totally understand everything you're saying. For some reason the truth seemed to be blocked concerning him. You have been the first person to ever speak the truth about him. Please don't give up on me. I can do this. I want to do this.

— Cindy

Dear Rob,

I'm crying again, and I haven't even started typing. Yes, the cleric is a dangerous man. I can still hear his voice and see his eyes. They both frighten me beyond belief. In the beginning, I was more wrong than he was. I pursued him. He didn't pursue me.

I knew he was looking down my blouse when I bent over, and I wanted him to, because I knew how he felt about women. I knew that would make him like me. I already performed a sacrilege by doing that. I never could face it before. That was just the beginning of many such instances. Why *wouldn't* he think he could have his way with me? I wanted him to like me so I could work in his ministry. I used tactics from the dark side to get close to him. How sick is that? Talk about mixed up.

I lusted in my heart, even if I didn't admit it in my mind. I just never thought he would take it that far. That's when I got scared, and that's when our relationship got even more intense. That's when the kindness and berating started. I used to think he loved me like a sister, until he just dismissed me like a car he was tired of driving. I said no to him, and *no* wasn't a word he liked or tolerated.

How do I take you and Jesus back there with me and get healed from this experience? I keep reading what you wrote earlier, but somehow I think I'm not going deep enough. I think I'm too scared to feel it, and scared to have what happened last night, happen again.

— Cindy

Chapter Eleven

Dear Rob,

As I'm sitting here praying, I swear I heard the Lord say, "Tell him about the other instance." It was more awful mentally. The night in the convent put the fear of God in me, but this other instance put the fear of the cleric in me.

I told you he used to berate me something terrible. This time, he did it in public, in front of everyone. It hurt me so badly that I thought I was going to die on the spot. Worse, we were giving him a surprise birthday party that night, and I had to act as though everything was fine all evening.

It was the longest and hardest night of my life. All I wanted to do was get away from him, but I had to sit by him and act like I loved him. To make matters worse, he made somebody on the plane switch places with me, and I had to sit next to him for ten hours.

The words and the humiliation are still in my heart. I'm feeling sick just thinking about it. I had to pretend in front of everybody that everything was all right, when all I wanted to do was cry my heart out and get away from him. I think, to this day, that's why I'm so afraid of confrontation. I was somebody, until he did that to me. Then I was a nobody, a bad nobody.

When I got home, I ended up in and out of the hospital for months. They couldn't find out what was wrong with me. They even sent me to Mayo, where they diagnosed me with Fibromyalgia. They even told me that trauma is usually what brings it on.

I know the day he yelled at me is when I got sick. I have never felt completely well ever since. Before that I was always thin and athletic. Now, I'm not. I have pain every day of my life, and fatigue, because of what this man did to me. I never wanted to admit this before, because then I would have to take responsibility for being with him in the first place, and letting all these dark events into my life.

I think this is where a lot of the anger towards him comes from. I told myself that if I ever got away from him, I would never go back, and I never did. That was the beginning of the end. When I wouldn't go to see him anymore, he got mad and released me.

— Cindy

Dear Rob,

I'm really trying to do this, but I keep getting a feeling that you're mad and disappointed in me. You can tell me if you are. I'm sorry I was such a mess last night and this morning. I really couldn't seem to help it. I guess I could have helped it if I would have fought.

Please say you forgive me. I won't ever do it again. I just need to know you're still with me. Something seems to be off even though I'm coming up with some good insight. I think it's because you're mad at me, and I don't want you to be mad at me.

— Cindy

Dear Rob,

Jesus breaks down the door and yells, "Get off of her! Let her go!" Jesus rushes over and pulls the man off of her. He puts his cloak around young Cindy, and sweeps her up into his arms. He turns to the cleric and says, "You are never to come near her again! She belongs to me."

I'm walking in front of Jesus, and you are in back. All the sisters are staring in disbelief. Jesus is so strong. He has come to take her home. He holds her so tight as he carries her out. She hears his Sacred Heart beating fast, because he is so angry. She is shaking like a leaf. He sits her down in the chapel. He still has his arm around her. She is still shaking.

She knows he's angry at the cleric, but she thinks he's angry at her, too. She can't even look him in his eyes. She just looks down at the ground, sobbing. He gently puts his hands on her cheeks and lifts her face to look in his eyes.

"I forgive you. I love you. I will take you home now, if you let me."

"Oh, Jesus, more than anything I want to go with you, but I feel so ashamed, and I'm still afraid of the cleric."

"He has no power over you. I will protect you."

"Can you really forgive me for everything?"

"I forgive you for everything. Let's go home now." He picks her up and carries her out. No one comes after them, and they never return to that place again.

— Cindy

Dear Cindy,

Your response was good, but I would like to see you get out of your head, away from your fears and into your heart. Go into your heart and get back into the scene. Do you remember the convent scene? Young Cindy is still being molested by evil. She is paralyzed with fear. She needs your help.

Do you remember Jesus' love when he delivered you from the hospital? It's the same Jesus — the God of love and mercy. All you need to do is be sorry for your sins and confess them to him. Then bring the forgiveness process to completion by accepting his love.

Your fear of punishment is keeping you from accepting Jesus' love.

Please go back into the imagination technique and shove the pervert off young Cindy. Take her by the hand. Let's run down the hall and into the chapel. He is waiting for you, little Cindy. He misses you. He wants you to come home. He has a great feast prepared in your honor. He will remove your rags of guilt and shame and dress you with the finest garments.

What are you waiting for? Invite Jesus into the scene and be reconciled with your heavenly Father.

— Rob

Dear Rob,

I can't believe you hit the nail on the head with one sentence. "Your fear of punishment is keeping you from accepting Jesus' love." I couldn't believe it when I read it. This is a huge breakthrough for me.

I was so tired last night that I could hardly type. I stayed with it until 1:30 a.m. trying, but I just couldn't get there. I will keep working on it today. I'll work on it by journaling and hopefully, I'll be able to come up with a better scenario from my heart. At least I finally understand. Thank you so much. God bless you for being so patient with me.

— Cindy

Dear Rob,

It sounds like a wolf is attacking a little lamb!

Jesus throws the door open and says, "I'm here for my daughter. She is my child, not yours! She belongs to me!"

He picks the man up and throws him across the room. Jesus looks over at Cindy. She has tears of fear in her eyes; not just fear of the cleric, but of Jesus, too. She is so afraid Jesus doesn't love her anymore because of her involvement with this man. Her greatest fear is that Jesus will turn his back on her and leave her, too. She's always afraid of being alone. The man knows this, and he is still looking at her.

The man says, "You were not alone when you were with me."

Jesus turns around and tells the man to keep silent.

The man turns to the girl and says, "You left him because he didn't love you. If he really loved you, why did he let so many people hurt you? Why didn't your parents ever love you? Jesus allowed all that to happen. I took you in when nobody else would."

Jesus is really mad now. He goes over and tapes the man's filthy mouth shut. He can hardly get the tape to stay on because there are so many worms coming out of the cleric's mouth.

The man jumps up and grabs for Cindy. He has a tight grip, and she can't get free. She looks at Jesus and says, "If you really love me, get him off of me!"

Jesus grabs the beast and throws him on the ground. Now maggots are all over the man. Jesus takes chains and he binds him. Finally, she is free.

Now Cindy is more frightened of Jesus than of the man. She can't stop thinking thoughts like, "Why did you let bad things happen to me? Why didn't you save me? Is it because I'm flawed from the beginning, a reject? I couldn't stand the thought of you rejecting me, too."

She is afraid Jesus is going to get mad at her. She turns over to try to escape his gaze and to hide her half-naked body. Shame and guilt fill her to overflowing. She is shaking with fear. It's dark, so very dark. She has always been afraid of the dark.

The first thing Jesus does is light a candle. He walks over and puts a beautiful white robe all around her. He caresses her hair and says, "Please don't cry, my little one. Do not be afraid. You never became a wolf. You stayed my little lamb; but you have many wounds. Man and beasts have attacked you, and even under attack, you did not become one of them. I know you cried a thousand tears. I caught every one of them before they hit the ground. I was always with you. The darkness was all around you, it's true; but I did not let it come into you. I chose you to be a special lamb for all eternity."

Cindy is still crying and shaking. She is afraid that if she opens her eyes and looks into Jesus' eyes, she will see a look of disappointment and disapproval, because she left the chapel and went into the dark room in the first place.

Jesus just keeps walking. You are walking in front of him, Rob, leading the way. No one dares to get in our way or say anything. We are on our way to the light, and nothing and no one is going to stop us!

You open the door, and Jesus carries me in. He lets me stay on his lap and keeps his arms around me tight. I love the feel of his hair on my face. Finally, I stop shaking. Jesus doesn't do anything. He just sits there holding me tight, protecting me. We sit there like that for a really long time. I can feel his love coming out of him into me. I can feel his mercy through his hair that lies on my face.

All fear leaves me. I open my eyes and I look into his and say, "I'm sorry Jesus. I'm so, so sorry."

Jesus says, "I know. It's OK. Really, it's OK. I forgive you. I forgive you for yesterday, I forgive you for today, and I will love you tomorrow."

— Cindy

Good work, Cindy!

Your letter made me cry. It also made my day.

— Thank you, Rob

Chapter Twelve

Dear Rob,

I ran across a box of personal stuff the cleric had given me — photos, letters, cards, his family pictures, tapes he gave me and books he wrote in. I was going to throw everything in the trash, but now I'm getting all these thoughts like, *I'm going to go to hell for criticizing a priest.*

There are pictures of him in formation ceremonies, conferences, Medjugorje, the Holy Land. I don't know what to do. Should I throw the pictures away? They are the only things I have from those places. I thought it was over, but I can't quit shaking. How can this man still hurt me like this after all these years? I never wanted anything from him in my new house, and now there's a box full of stuff.

I wish I had a match to burn it all. I knew I was getting ready to come under attack. I even went to two Masses today and prayed in front of the Blessed Sacrament. I keep asking the Blessed Mother to help me. I'd thought I better e-mail you, too. Please pray for me.

— Cindy

Dear Cindy,

I want to put an end to this "going to hell" thing. Who said you were going to go to hell? Did your parents say that when you were little? Who said you can't say something bad about an unhealthy priest?

God alone decides who is going to heaven or hell. It's not my place to guarantee anyone's salvation, or to cast anyone into the outer darkness, because I'm not God.

I don't worry about hell because I know when I'm in right relationship with God and when I'm not. I keep my focus on God, and I keep my life focused on pleasing God. I maintain a close relationship with God every day, and it's in that relationship that my trust rests. When I keep my relationship tight and strong, there's no need to worry about hell. I hope this puts an end to the hell thing.

In regards to the box full of the cleric's trash, you will need to look to the Lord for guidance. I think you and the Lord need to go through it bit by bit and continue to confess and repent until you have peace. I'm sure some of it needs to be denounced and destroyed, but even if you burn it with fire, in no way are you disrespecting the Holy Land. You are only breaking unhealthy soul-ties and repenting from past sins.

I'm glad the Lord showed you the box of goodies. I would like to see you work through one of the cleric's berating scenes. Instead of having Jesus protect you, I would like to see you defend yourself. I would like to see you confront the cleric's lies with the truth and start acting more assertively.

If the Lord wants you to act more assertively in real life, it may be a good idea to learn lessons and get training from your past experiences. Where is this cleric now? Is he still forcing women to have sex with him? Maybe the Lord wants someone to take action and put an end to this man's sickness.

— Rob

Dear Rob,

The hell thing was drilled into me when I was a child. The one who really scared me to death with it was the cleric — especially about not ever criticizing a priest.

I felt bad enough throwing the books away, but he had written in them, so they had to go. The pictures I put to the side. I was going to throw them away, but they are all I have of the Holy Land. Unfortunately, he is in almost every one of them. Do you think I could keep the ones that he's not in, if there are any?

The pictures were of good memories, not bad. Lots are with my family. He came and stayed with us sometimes. We were just close to him, as we have been close to many priests and nuns.

I have this battle going on inside of me. Is the cleric bad or good? I really don't know. I know that if there's just one drop of poison in a cup of water, the water is poisonous. The cleric seemed to do a lot of good deeds. I have focused on the bad with you, but the good parts are messing up my mind about the bad parts.

I feel like I had open-heart surgery the other day and I still have a lot of healing to do. I just need someone to tell me the truth. All my life, nobody has ever wanted to talk about anything. We had to keep my visit to the mental ward quiet and my out-of-wedlock pregnancy quiet. I grew up in silent shame. Even my spiritual director didn't want me talking about what happened with the cleric.

— Cindy

Dear Rob,

I found the cleric's biography in one of the boxes, and a lot of it probably isn't true. He used to say that he had worked with Mother Teresa, but when I sent her some of his tapes he got really mad. I also heard the Jesuits let him go before he came to the United States. I don't know if it's true or not.

The more I get into this, the more I realize the spiritual danger. I keep thinking of the fruit. There was so much bad fruit, especially to my mental state, not to mention my soul. There was some good fruit, like when he taught me a lot of stuff about the Blessed Mother. Then again, he also destroyed my spiritual well-being and made me afraid of priests.

I haven't found all the Holy Land pictures yet. I just found the ones that were in the boxes with all his other stuff. There are still boxes of pictures somewhere. I will keep looking.

— Cindy

Dear Rob,

Concerning the pictures — I shake to hold them. I can't get his face out of my mind. How could I even think to keep them, except that there's a lot of pictures of him with my precious family? There are a lot of pictures of friends and places in the Holy Land that I treasure as well. I felt as though I would be throwing them away, too. That's the part that's hard for me.

I have to get this clear in my mind: Is he involved in evil or not? Do I need to get rid of all the pictures, even if he's not in them? I don't care if I don't have any pictures of the Holy Land or Medjugorje, or if I have to let go of the pictures of my precious family. If that's what it takes to be rid of any evil residue, I'm serious. Nothing is worth anything if it would hurt me because it's associated with evil.

— Cindy

Dear Cindy,

Repressing all this stuff and not talking about it is not healthy. The Lord wants his people to acknowledge their sins and bring them into the light to be forgiven. You have confessed your sins, and you are forgiven, but for some reason, you are not completely free. I want you to ask the Lord to break all unhealthy ties with this situation. This may take some time. These ties were formed over many years, and you can't expect them to go away overnight.

Part of your bondage is trying to judge the cleric as good or evil. I'm sure the man does some good works. You have also testified about some of his bad works. Humans are spiritual vessels. We do both good and bad things. God alone is judge, and God will judge the cleric. It's not my place to say he's good or bad, nor is it your place.

Because you are still shaking when you hold the pictures and can't get his face out of your mind, I believe you are still held in bondage and the Lord is working to set you free. You need to go to the Lord and see what he has to say. How is your quiet time going?

Release the cleric to the Lord. Cut all unhealthy soul-ties and bonds. Ask the Lord about your pictures. It sounds like you are hanging on to stuff again — that somehow the stuff will make you feel loved; that somehow the pictures will make you feel more valuable; that somehow pictures of your family will make your family more... Please fill in the blank here.

I don't see Jesus hoarding all kinds of stuff. I don't read about the time when Jesus entered the town of Samaria and started collecting souvenirs. He didn't fill his pockets full of special rocks to help him remember the fun times. He didn't take a hundred roles of film to capture the precious moments.

The Bible says that *love never ends.* Jesus was too busy loving people. Love lasts forever. The love Jesus allowed to enter his heart and to flow from his heart lasts forever. You can't take anything with you. It is all going to burn. None of your stuff, souvenirs or family pictures will make it into heaven. Love is the only video recording you can take into heaven. Are you loading up boxes of firewood, or are you storing up heavenly treasure?

— Rob

Dear Rob,

You are right. I'm trying to hold on to stuff again. I have read your letter several times and have dropped everything I was doing to have as much quiet time as possible from here on out.

I took everything and bagged it up. There were three big trash bags. I could hardly carry them. I took them to the church and put them in Jesus' trash can and said, "I give this to you." Then I went to Adoration chapel for a long time. I kept one picture and note to give Jesus in front of the Blessed Sacrament. I tore them up in front of him and gave them to him directly.

All is in the trash — all the pictures, all the notes, the books, the gifts, everything. I even threw away the rosary and crucifix from India and asked the Lord to forgive me. If something bad was attached, I didn't want it to hurt anybody else. There are more pictures somewhere. I tried to find them, but couldn't. All that I found are in the trash. Jesus' trash, literally.

I prayed for a long time in front of the Blessed Sacrament. Here's what the Lord spoke to me when I was writing in my journal:

You must come to me daily. I will keep filling you up with me – my love, my peace, my freedom, which comes only from surrendering everything and everybody to me. When you give something to me, it will make an opening for more of me to come into you.

I know you are hurting and bleeding. Come daily and receive my body into your body. Open yourself up completely and entirely. Make yourself available to me.

You've been looking for love in all the wrong places. Come to me. Do not let anything or anybody keep you from me. I give my healing hand to you. I will stop your blood from flowing. I will fill your empty heart with my presence. You just have to make room by getting rid of everything that is not of me.

After the Lord gave me these words, I've decided that I will make it a top priority to get to daily Mass and make a Holy Hour every day.

— Cindy

Chapter Thirteen

Dear Cindy,

Good job at getting rid of the stuff at the Lord's house.

Will you please consider writing a healing letter about your parents condemning you to hell when you were a child? I don't know what happened, but I would like to hear about it. I realize it's a small item compared to the other healing issues we have been dealing with, but it's important to deal with it and remove it from your soul.

As small as it may seem, it had the power to trip you up when we were working on the convent scene. The enemy was using it against you, and it came up several times in our conversations.

Here's what I would like you to do. Write a letter telling your parents how and why it's wrong to shame and scare a child with thoughts of hell. Tell your parents that Jesus loves little children. Try to dig up any anger that you have towards your parents and let them hear about it.

After the first letter is written, I want you to write an apology letter on your parents' behalf. Picture them in a completely healed state full of God's love and write, on their behalf, the most loving words of apology that you deserve to hear.

Please put your emotions into it. By doing so, you will be removing another brick in the wall of shame that has been built around your heart.

— Rob

P.S. I'm also glad to hear about your commitment to spend more time in Adoration. It looks like the Lord is already starting to speak to you in profound ways.

Dear Mom,

All during my childhood, I was afraid of doing something wrong and getting in trouble. Getting in trouble meant lots of yelling, being slapped a few times, and being told how bad a person I was. You told me that so much, I still believe it today.

Even though I want to be loved, I don't feel deserving of love, and I have never felt secure — never, not with anybody, not even with God. When I feel unpleasing to God, I feel I must be going to hell. You even told me I was going to hell for hurting you and for all the sins I had committed. I really thought I was a bad seed. You told me that enough, and I grew up believing it.

I also remember the times you said you wished I was never born. I used to wish it, too. I saw how miserable you were, and I used to think it was all my fault. I thought God was going to punish me for hurting you and making your life so miserable. All I ever wanted was for you to like me, but you made me cry at every important event.

I remember the one and only birthday party you ever gave me. I was so excited. I was eight years old, and I was having my first birthday party. I couldn't believe everybody was bringing presents and coming to see me.

What did you do? You took me to the side and told me all the things I was doing wrong and how much I was embarrassing you. After that I didn't want to go back to the party. I just wanted everybody to go home.

All I ever wanted to do was please you, but I never could. Nothing was ever good enough, or done the way you wanted.

My whole life you told me how wrong I was. I couldn't dance, I couldn't write, I didn't know how to pick out clothes and no one would ever want me. I was a constant embarrassment to you.

You used to tell me you were going to divorce Daddy, and that it was my fault. I would try to be so good because I didn't want Daddy to leave. I would end up crying, and when I told him what you said, you said I was lying. He believed you, not me. You also threatened to kill yourself if I didn't do exactly what you said. How is a kid supposed to deal with that kind of pressure?

I started living in a fantasy world. I would do anything to escape reality. All I ever thought about was getting away before you did something bad, to prevent it from being my fault. Guess what? All the things you said about me came into me. They are still with me to this day.

You have never wanted anyone to love me. I know you did this out of your own pain, and maybe your mother did it to you. Guess what? Your words came true. I have failed, and I know God is going to punish me for not being a better child, a better teenager, a better wife, a better mother and a better grandmother.

I want to be good for God, but I don't know how to be good, because no one ever taught me that I was good, or that I could be loved, or that I deserved to be loved. Guess what, Mom, everything you ever said about me came true. I'm the mess you always said I would be.

— Your broken daughter, Cindy

My Dearest Daughter Cindy,

I'm sorry for all the times I hurt you. I know how hard you tried to please me, but nothing you ever did was right. It wasn't your fault, Cindy. You were a good little girl. You brought so much joy to my heart when you were born. I did want you. It's just that I was a child having a child.

I had my own insecurities to deal with. We had to live with your grandparents. We were so poor. I'm sure I blamed you for a lot of things. I shouldn't have done that to you. It wasn't your fault.

Everybody thought you were so cute. But when they loved you, I felt they didn't love me. That's the reason I fought you from the day you were born. I wanted the love that you received from others. I wanted to be loved, too. I was miserable and I took it out on you.

I'm sorry, Cindy. I'm so sorry I didn't tell you how pretty and sweet and good you were. I know I did all this to you. I'm sorry. I'm really sorry. Please forgive me.

— Love, Mom

Dear Cindy,

Good job writing the healing letter! It looks like the Lord showed you a lot of good insight. Here's what I would like you to do next. Please go to Adoration chapel, picture your mom standing before Jesus, and then release your mom to the Lord.

Please say these words to your mom and add your own words as well: "You are no longer my responsibility! I send you to Jesus. I'm no longer obligated to make you happy. I'm no longer responsible for your happiness. It's not my fault that you are unhappy.

"I'm no longer responsible for your life, your decisions, or problems. I release you to the Lord Jesus! I break all your guilt and shame! I break all unhealthy soul-ties between you and me. I break all curses that you have spoken against me.

"I send back all your hurtful and abusive words, and I ask Jesus to forgive you. I ask Jesus to replace all the hurtful words and sickness that you have inflicted upon me with a blessing of his love and forgiveness.

"You are no longer my god. I will never again live to please you as my lord. I'm free to be loved. I am free to love and serve the Lord. I am free to accept the Lord's love. I am free to accept love from others."

After you say all this, ask the Lord if there is anything else he wants to show you. Ask him if there is anything else you need to release. After big Cindy releases your mom to the Lord, I want little Cindy to say the same words.

Take little Cindy in your arms and have her break all your

mom's curses and send back all her guilt. Little Cindy needs to be free from all bondage. When you are all finished, leave your mom in Jesus' love and care.

— Rob

Dear Rob,

I just got home from church — what an incredible heart-wrenching encounter! It was kind of the Lord to not let anybody come in while I was sitting there bawling and doing this with him. What a release, what a relief. I felt guilty for telling you about my mother, but now I'm OK, because I left her with Jesus.

Here are some of the highlights from my conversation with the Lord:

You always thought the fights between your parents were about you. That's why you take everything so personally. You always think that when others are mad, sad or busy, they are angry with you, and that you have done something wrong.

I want to release you from this responsibility. You are not responsible for other people's actions. Let others assume responsibility for their own actions. Even if you do something that causes another person to react, turn the situation over to me and I will let my light of truth pour through you.

My grace is upon all who turn to me. I want to mend your heart completely. I want to take away all your guilt and shame. I want to break all the bonds that are holding you. I will take all the shaming and hurtful words from your memory and replace them with my love.

I release you from the feelings of rejection. These too I take away from you. I replace them with a certainty that I am with you always and I want you to be with me always. Never will I leave you. Never will I reject you. There is nothing you could say or do to make me not love you completely and entirely. As you love your children and grandchildren, so I love you, my dearest child, Cindy.

— Thanks again, Cindy

Dear Cindy,

Good job releasing your mom and listening to the Lord. Are you ready for more healing work? Do you want to work on your family situation next? How is your fast going?

— Rob

Dear Rob,

I've asked the Lord about fasting several times, and I believe he wants me to go 40 days like he did in the wilderness. I want to do it for him, too. Some days are harder than others. When I start feeling down, I still want to eat. But I haven't, and I won't.

I think I should work on my family situation, even though I'm scared to. I don't know if I have the strength. I'm afraid of what you might ask me to do. I'm not good at talking to them about anything. I just try to stay out of everybody's way and do what they tell me to do.

I've had to really fight to be able to keep going to daily Mass and make Holy Hours. They don't mind me spending time with the Lord, but only as long as it doesn't interfere with what they want me to do for them.

I'm probably making them sound worse than they are. I have conditioned them to treat me like this. It's not their fault. I have never thought I had the right to make my own decisions about anything, and when I try, all hell breaks loose. When it does, I usually retreat, because I can't bear confrontation. I don't know if that means I need more past healing work to get stronger, or if I need to work on the way I interact with my family.

I think you would know the answer to that better than I would. I'll do whatever you think. I just want to keep going towards the light and out of the darkness. Looking back, I can't believe where I was 25 days ago, compared to where I'm at now. I would have never thought that I could fast on vegetables, water and decaf tea, not to mention visit the painful places in my memory. This is truly miraculous to me. I'm not jumping ship now. Whatever you think is best, that's what I will do next.

— Cindy

Dear Cindy,

I like the idea of a 40-day fast. Let me know your completion date, and I will pray for your strength to see it through.

I will also pray about your family situation. Don't worry about an external confrontation. We will work on your internal ability to be more assertive. Once your internal work is complete, your internal strength will automatically flow into your external environment.

— Rob

Dear Rob,

My 40th day of fasting will be on August 13. I will break the fast on August 14, the Feast of St. Maximilian Kolbe, and the eve of the Assumption of the Blessed Virgin Mary.

I think it was kind of the Blessed Mother to have me break it on the Feast of St. Maximilian Kolbe, because I consecrated myself to Jesus through Mary on that date. This was the original reason I got involved with the cleric in the first place. I didn't realize the date until I looked it up to tell you.

— Cindy

Chapter Fourteen

Dear Cindy,

We know the cleric was involved with alternative forms of spirituality, so when you told me about the consecration prayer you said with him, I found myself very concerned. There are some extremely destructive consecration prayers that are ensnaring many religious souls these days.

I also forgot to ask you about your family's involvement with alternative forms of spirituality. Have you ever visited a palm reader? Did you ever play with a Ouija board? Do you have any Freemasons, Mormons or witches in your family lineage? What about any New Age involvement, or joining groups like Rainbow Girls, or have you made any other secret vows? Please take a prayerful look at your past as well as your parents' and grandparents' pasts.

Please describe what happened with the consecration prayer and your introduction with the cleric. I want you to denounce and break all unhealthy spiritual vows that are not of the Lord. Many vows and agreements seem harmless when you are making them, but if they are not clean before the Lord, the devil can acquire a foothold in your soul and cause all kinds of problems.

— Rob

Dear Rob,

I made the consecration prayer, through the Blessed Mother, the St. Louis de Montfort way. You say prayers for 33 days in preparation, and then say the consecration prayer on the 33rd day. The cleric prayed over me, so I don't know if he said something in private, different from what I was saying.

This is why I originally went to see the cleric in the first place. I wanted to consecrate myself to Jesus through the Blessed Mother. At the time, I thought the cleric was the only one offering this type of dedication.

He had me sit in front of the Blessed Sacrament literally all day and write the prayer over and over. He said by nighttime I would mean what I was writing. I did mean it. I loved Jesus and Mother Mary, and I wanted to belong to both of them. Here is the prayer that I said:

O Eternal and Divine Wisdom,

Ungrateful and faithless as I have been, I have not kept the promises that I made so solemnly to thee in my baptism; I have not fulfilled my obligations; I do not deserve to be called thy child, nor yet thy slave; and there is nothing in me which does not merit thy anger and thy repulse.

I dare not come by myself before thy most holy and august Majesty. It is on this account that I have recourse to the intercession of thy most holy Mother, whom thou hast given me for a mediatrix with thee. It is through her that I hope to obtain of thee contrition and the pardon of my sins.

Therefore I, _________, a faithless sinner, renew and ratify today in thy hands the vows of my baptism. In the presence of all the heavenly court I choose thee this day for my Mother and Mistress. I deliver and consecrate to thee, as thy slave, my body and soul, my goods, both interior and exterior, and even the value of all my good actions, past, present and future; leaving to thee the entire and full right of disposing of me, and all that belongs to me, without exception.

To my knowledge, no one in my family has ever been involved in anything like you mentioned. I played with a Ouija board and eight-ball as a child. I also remember playing like I could read palms, and I might have had somebody read my palm once.

I used to read all kinds of self-help books. Once I found out how dangerous New Age books were, I stopped reading them. I also remember visiting a store that had crystals. I don't think I bought anything. I remember feeling cold in there and I wanted to leave. I used to not know about all this stuff. I got really scared when I found out it was all powered by fallen angels.

My grandfather might have been involved with the Shriners. Aren't they associated with Freemasons?

The cleric had this thing with numbers. For the longest time, I acquired this compulsion from him to buy or do things in certain numbers. He would always say that everything you do should mean something and have a connection. For example, if I were buying soap, I would have to buy seven bars, for the seven gifts of the Holy Spirit.

I thought he was helping me be more spiritual, but for the

longest time, I had this obsessive compulsion. If I heated up food, I had to heat it up for a certain amount of time that connected to something spiritual. It drove me crazy. If I wanted to buy something, and I couldn't find the right number, I didn't think I could buy it. I didn't even know how to determine what the number should be.

I will keep praying about this. If I come up with anything else, I will let you know.

— Cindy

Dear Cindy,

We like to think of Satan as a fool for getting kicked out of heaven, but I would like for you to think of the devil as a brilliant trial lawyer. He used to be one of the Lord's most intelligent creatures, and I can assure you that the devil is extremely cunning and crafty.

The devil will try to trick humans into making agreements and vows so that he can use them against us. If the devil can't get us to utter a vow when we're angry, he will draft his own version and trick us through our prayers. All he needs is a little word play, a switch of identity trick.

For example, there's a false prophet in the Bible named Bar-Jesus. Jesus is also a popular Spanish name. If it's possible for a man to be named Jesus, the devil can also assign the name of Jesus to any one of his fallen angels.

There is only one Jesus of Nazareth *who came in the flesh*, and that is why 1 John 4: 1–4 tells us to test all spirits to make sure they are from God. Any spirit that can confess truth before the Lord Jesus Christ of Nazareth *who came in the flesh* is from God. When testing the spirits, I usually add the words, *by the power of his blood, his cross and his resurrection*, just to make sure I'm dealing with the real Jesus.

Do you see why testing the spirits is important?

If Satan can't trick you into making a vow that will cut you off from God, he will draft his own version and get you to pray it. For example, the consecration prayer you said: *I deliver and consecrate to thee, as thy slave, my body and soul, my goods, both interior and exterior, and even the value of all my good actions, past, present and future; leaving to thee the entire and full right of disposing of me, and all that belongs to me, without exception.*

These types of vows are dangerous because all Satan has to do is assign a demon the name Immaculata or Divine Wisdom, and trick a human into dedicating their life and soul into its possession for all eternity. Who is Immaculata? Is it a demon? Is it a pagan goddess? Is it Mary Queen of Heaven? In Jeremiah 44, demons were operating under the name of Queen of Heaven.

Do you see why testing the spirits is extremely important? Demons are filthy liars. If demons can be assigned the name Jesus, or Queen of Heaven, they can also be assigned the name, Immaculata or Divine Wisdom.

How do you know that you didn't dedicate yourself to a religious spirit as its possession and property for all eternity? Did you test the spirits before dedicating yourself to an unknown entity? Did you have Jesus' permission before praying such a prayer?

Here are some things I would like for you to consider in regards to the consecration prayer you made with the cleric: What was wrong with your original baptism vows? Why would you ratify them and place them into the hands of a spiritual entity named Divine Wisdom?

I want you to study the words of the vow you prayed and show me some examples from Jesus' life when he treated people with that kind of contempt. *I do not deserve to be called thy child, nor yet thy slave; and there is nothing in me which does not merit thy anger and thy repulse.* Take a look at how Jesus treated Mary Magdalene and Matthew the tax collector, and then please explain the words of this vow to me.

Why would you dedicate yourself to a saint, anyway? The saints in heaven are no different than the saints here on earth. Sure, they are closer to God and they have the ability to intercede for us, but we still should not be doing anything with the saints in heaven that we would not do with the saints here on earth.

The real Jesus wants all of you. Jesus wants to heal all your hurts. Jesus wants to clean you up physically, spiritually and emotionally. He wants no false gods before him. He wants no saints before him. He wants no earthly humans before him. Jesus wants your full dedication and devotion. He wants you to fulfill the first and greatest commandment. He wants you to love him with your whole heart, mind, body and soul. He wants to enter a deep, rich and passionate relationship with you.

— Rob

Dear Rob,

I have read your letter at least ten times, and I'm not sure I understand what you are saying. I totally get that we need to test the spirits. My spiritual director used to say that to me all the time.

I don't know Scripture like you do, and I'm not sure I understand all the words of the consecration. I do love the Blessed Mother, and I thought I gave myself to Jesus *through* her, not *to* her. Are you saying Satan can somehow block that and assign a religious spirit in its place? Are you saying I may have dedicated myself to an evil spirit instead of to Jesus?

I totally want what you said in the last paragraph of your letter. I want a real relationship with the Lord, and I don't want any false gods before him. I'm just mixed up on what you are saying. Please tell me what I have to do to stay on the right road and have that kind of relationship with the real Jesus.

— Cindy

Dear Cindy,

You still haven't answered my question. What was wrong with your original baptism vows? Why would you want to change or ratify your baptism vows?

I know Satan hates Catholic baptism vows, especially when prayed over young children. It's through these vows that we receive the gift of the Holy Spirit. The vows are powerful and effective. It's easy to see why Satan would want everybody to change their vows and consecrate themselves to unknown spiritual entities, especially when they don't understand the words they are praying.

In Matthew 10:37 Jesus says, *Whoever loves father or mother more than me is not worthy of me; and whoever loves son or daughter more than me is not worthy of me.* Would this apply to our heavenly mothers, brothers and sisters, too? Does this apply to everything? Are you required to love the Lord your God with your entire heart, mind, body and soul and to have no false gods before him?

In doing your healing work, we are discovering that you feel unworthy of Jesus. Deep in your heart you are scared of Jesus and somehow feel cut off from Jesus. Do you love the Blessed Mother more than Jesus? If so, you have set up a false god in your heart.

I want you to search your heart and answer these questions. What's preventing you from dedicating yourself fully to Christ? No middlemen, no other lovers, no secret vows or promises, totally and fully devoted and consecrated to Christ!

I look forward to hearing what you and the Lord come up with. Please seek the Lord with all diligence in the matter. Whatever it is, let's deal with it and move on to the next step in your healing journey.

— Rob

Dear Rob,

Now I understand what you are saying. You have brought up a lot of valid and important points. Last night I felt so confused. This morning I understand much better. I want to be completely and entirely consecrated to the Lord. I want to get to know the Lord more deeply. I don't want to be afraid of him anymore. I want to serve him. I want to love him. I want to feel his love for me. I want no false gods before him.

To answer your question, the only things stopping me from dedicating myself fully to Jesus have been my feelings of unworthiness and the fear of rejection. I just keep going to Mass and spending time with him in front of the Blessed Sacrament. I'm praying to get past all my emotional baggage and open the doors wide for him to come into my heart.

I still feel unworthy, and I still fear rejection, but these are just feelings. I've been giving these feelings to him and asking him to help me in whatever ways I need. I want to know him more, to love him more, and to serve him with all my heart, mind, body and soul.

— Cindy

Dear Cindy,

I know you profess your love for Christ, but who have you been running to for comfort? In the past you ran to food for comfort. That would make food a false god.

When it comes to prayer, who are you running to for comfort? If you spend more time praying to Mary than Jesus, does that make Mary a false God? If you spend more time watching television than communing with God in prayer, is that another false god? If you are running to a counselor or spiritual director for comfort, instead of Jesus, is that person a false god, too?

The job of a good counselor is to connect people with God. I don't have any spiritual power of my own. It all comes from God. When people latch onto me, make me their god and try to suck spiritual power out of me in an attempt to make themselves feel better, all it does is drain me and leave us both depleted. I get my spiritual power and strength from the Lord. I help people by connecting them to the source of all power, God.

The saints in heaven work the same way. Saint Paul is not up in heaven fighting for your attention. He doesn't want you to make him into a false god. Saint Paul wants you to get connected to the real God. The same is true with Mary. Mary does not want you to worship her and cry out to her day and night. Mary wants you to get connected with her Son.

If you have given your spiritual director a more prominent place in your heart than Jesus, I would want you to surrender that place in your heart to Jesus. If you have given Mary a more prominent place in your heart than Jesus, she would want you to surrender that place in your heart to Jesus. Mary wants to connect you with her Son.

Can you do this, Cindy? Do you see what I'm talking about? Do you agree with this? You will also need to denounce the Ouija board, any lies you may have picked up while reading New Age books and any involvement with the palm reader. If your grandfather's involvement with the Shriners has exposed you to a generational curse, you will need to break that agreement, too.

— Rob

Dear Rob,

Yes, I can do this. I do understand what you are talking about, with all of it. Some of it is hard to hear, but I understand and I agree with everything.

— Cindy

Dear Cindy,

After going to bed, the Lord prompted me to get up and write this to you. Please take it under prayerful consideration. The question I would like to ask you, have you ever had a spirit-filled encounter with the Lord?

I talk about my spiritual awakening with the Lord in the 12th chapter of *Journey of Endurance.* I opened my heart up to Jesus and fell in love with him. It's what the Charismatic Catholics call being baptized with the gift of the Holy Spirit.

The best way to describe it is like falling in love with a romantic lover. It was the same function of my heart as falling in love with a girlfriend. If you have ever fallen in love, you know what I'm talking about. I had to capture the presence of who the woman was and accept her into my heart.

Everyone will have a different encounter with the Lord. Both Peter and Paul had their own unique encounters. Peter's occurred the day of Pentecost, and Paul experienced the Lord on the road to Damascus. Have you had this kind of encounter with Jesus? If not, I think the Lord has big plans for you.

After I invited Jesus into my heart I had the most euphoric week of closeness with him in my entire life. It was so powerful I would get overwhelmed after five minutes in prayer. The sweet intimacy was too much for me to endure.

All you need to do is surrender your heart. Capture the presence of who Christ is and invite him into your heart. Fall in love with Jesus like a romantic lover.

— Rob

Chapter Fifteen

Dear Rob,

I can't believe what you are saying to me. I'm ready, and I want this with all my heart! I went to the Blessed Sacrament last night for a long time, and I cried my heart out to him. I feel very open to him. I would be so grateful if this could happen. I want it so much! I'm crying now just thinking of it. It's all I've ever wanted.

— Cindy

Dear Cindy,

Ask God to show you the reason for the holdup. Are there any other false gods standing in your way? Have you completely surrendered everything? Are you holding anything back? Is there anything else you need to denounce? Have you denounced all vows and consecration prayers made to spiritual entities other than the one true God?

I will keep praying for you. I know you are very close to something really big.

— Rob

Dear Rob,

I think I have denounced everything. I had a tremendously wonderful experience at Holy Communion where I could feel the Sacred Heart inside my heart. It was awesome! Afterwards, I realized what was standing in the way of a complete surrender:

I talked myself into keeping more Holy Land pictures. I told you I would get rid of them, but when I found them, I wanted to keep them. I think this might be what is blocking the full experience.

I'm going to gather the pictures and throw them in Jesus' trash can. I'm shaking just holding them. I will go back in front of the Blessed Sacrament, and I'm not leaving until I get to where I need to be. I want this more than anything. I know I'm really close, and I'm not going to let Satan stop me.

— Cindy

Dear Rob,

I'm embarrassed to tell you this, but I wanted to bring it into the light. I wanted to keep the pictures, because I looked better then. I was thin. I looked like a woman, instead of a fat slob. Maybe that's the sin that's holding me back.

How could I even consider keeping the pictures? Just looking at them put me in a bad place again. Yet, I want to look at them one more time before I throw them away. What's wrong with me? I'm not going to bed tonight until this is finished. I really feel closer to the Sacred Heart of Jesus. I'm not at all afraid of him anymore, and can't believe I ever was. I want to be completely open to him. I want nothing and nobody between us.

— Cindy

Dear Rob,

It's done. I threw it all in Jesus' trash can at church. He even had me come back when I was almost to the church and get a ring my friend gave me while we were in Jerusalem. I used to wear it all the time and had forgotten about it.

I renounced everything I could think of and asked the Lord if there was anything else. I spent two hours in front of the Blessed Sacrament. We weren't alone, and that was part of the problem. People were working on the church and having meetings, coming in and out for a million things. That's what goes on at that church. They come in and out, but they don't spend any time with the Lord. It breaks my heart.

During the rest of the day, I kept feeling that the Lord wanted to give me much more, but that I was blocking it. I couldn't figure it out until I walked in the door just now. That's when he told me. He wants me to forgive myself.

I've made so many mistakes against him. I believe he forgives me, but I still can't believe I deserve to be forgiven. I was hoping that after I felt more of his divine presence, it would come, but I think he wants me to work on self-forgiveness first. How do I forgive myself when I know I deserve to go to hell? I don't want to go to hell, I want to be close to him. I'm stuck and torn between these two extremes.

— Cindy

Dear Cindy,

When you look at your past and start feeling bad, what events come to mind? What negative situations are you still holding on to? Let's identify these events and break them down into separate scenes. I will show you how to forgive yourself.

Send over one event that comes to mind. Tell me what happened. The young girl from your past made a mistake. What did she do?

— Rob

Dear Rob,

I let a boy come into my room at night while my parents were upstairs. We had sex. He is the father of the child that I had out of wedlock.

— Cindy

Dear Rob,

I don't know if I can do this. I'm so ashamed about what I told you already, and that's only the tip of the iceberg. If we have to go over each event, this could take a lifetime. It could suffice to say that I could have been St. Augustine's sister when I was 15 to 20 years old.

I lived an exceedingly promiscuous lifestyle. I just wanted to be loved. In those days, I thought having sex was love. I never felt loved or accepted by anybody. Then after all those years of sin, I got involved with the cleric. There wasn't much of anything in between.

When I think about all those years it feels like a knife in my heart. I think this is what the Lord feels because of all my sins. It breaks my heart that I have hurt him like this. If I had known, I would have never done it. I just didn't know him then. I thought I was only hurting myself, which was the whole purpose.

— Cindy

Dear Cindy,

Many years ago, I was running a backhoe trying to uncover a water main. I knew the water main was buried about five to six feet below grade. We needed to uncover several places to tap the line. My helper was inspecting the excavation. He had a shovel and probing rod and after he made sure the area was clear, I would remove another bucketful of dirt.

We worked hard all day and uncovered three places in the pipeline. It started getting dark, so we stopped for the evening. The next morning, I started the backhoe and after removing the first bucket of dirt, I hit the water main and broke a hole in the side of the pipe.

I was extremely mad at myself. I had ruptured an eight-inch water main that belonged to the Metropolitan District. If the line had not been shut off, it would have washed out the entire hillside. I had to call the water department and tell them what happened. I also had to call in an emergency repair crew to cut out a section of the pipe and repair the damage.

I want you to picture this scene. Adult Rob is extremely angry. He wants to blame someone, but his helper wasn't around when this happened. He only has himself to blame. Present-day Rob needs to forgive the guy who was running the backhoe.

To work through the self-forgiveness process, present-day Rob had to go back and understand past Rob. The two men needed to have a conversation. In this conversation, present-day Rob realized that past Rob didn't know the pipe was there. If past Rob knew the pipe was there, he would have been more careful. Past Rob didn't know any better. He was doing the best he could.

Once present-day Rob looked into past Rob's eyes, his heart began to soften. He realized past Rob and present-day Rob are on the same team. Past Rob would never rupture a water main intentionally. It was a mistake.

After realizing this, present-day Rob's heart began to soften even more. He was able to have compassion for past Rob. Past Rob felt terrible. He wanted to cry. The thought of paying for the damage made him feel even worse. How could present-day Rob be mad at past Rob any longer? Compassion for past Rob entered his heart. Past Rob needed love, support and encouragement. He didn't need anyone yelling at him. He needed love!

Once I came to that place of understanding, I was able to love myself and forgive myself.

Here's what I would like for you to do: go back in time using an imagination technique. I want adult Cindy to go back into young Cindy's room and have a talk with her and her boyfriend. I want you to tell them about the sacredness of our sexuality. Tell them why sex is reserved for the confines of marriage.

Tell them God designed sex to bond a couple together for a lifetime. Sex outside of a marriage commitment is wrong, because God doesn't want his children bonded together with the wrong person. Sex also leads to procreation. If a couple is not married in a God-approved loving union, then they should not bring children into this world.

I'm sure adult Cindy knows all these lessons, but I don't think young Cindy knew better. I want you to go back and educate young Cindy and her boyfriend on these topics. After you send the young man home, I want you to love little Cindy. She was probably hurting from her parents' neglect. She just wants someone to love her, to hold her, to pay attention to her.

I want you to love her, to hold her and to pay attention to her. I want you to go back and feel her pain and speak all the words that she needs to hear. Tell her she is valuable, beautiful and precious. Invite Jesus into the scene and introduce the young girl to Jesus. Allow Jesus' love to flow through you into the young girl's heart. If necessary, take her to a face-to-face confession with Jesus. Have Jesus look into her eyes and speak the words, *You are forgiven!* Have Jesus say them over and over. *You are forgiven.*

— Rob

Dear Rob,

I spent the last three hours in Adoration, and here's what happened: we're all in the room. Little Cindy just wants to be loved. It's all she ever wanted — to be loved by somebody. This boy holds her and wants to use her body. Hopefully he likes her a little bit, too. But at least he's holding her and paying attention to her. It makes her feel that she's worth something.

Jesus and adult Cindy walk into the room. Jesus is not angry, and after little Cindy looks into his eyes, she knows she must stop doing what she's doing. She must send the boy out of her room. After seeing Jesus, she wants to. She wants to go into his arms instead.

After the boy leaves, Jesus and I walk over and cover her naked body with his cloak. It's so warm and comforting. Jesus holds her so closely. Tears are streaming down his face because wolves have attacked his little lamb. She is trembling and crying incessantly. She tells the Lord she is so very sorry! He looks into her eyes and says, "I forgive you, little Cindy.

"I forgive you now and for all future nights when you go to other men besides me looking for what only I can give you. Wolves can't love you like I love you. They want to devour you like a predator who sees a lamb alone and trembling. It's what they know, it's what they do. They don't care about you. Their hearts do not belong to me, and therefore they cannot really love you like I do.

"I know you didn't know any better. So many times, in so many ways, you were just looking for me. You were lost in dark rooms where I could not come in to see you, and all that time, I always stood outside your door, always. Never did I leave you.

I could hear you inside crying out to me, but the door was locked, preventing me from getting inside to you. I cried many tears because I knew what the wolves were doing to you."

"But Lord," I said, "You are God. Couldn't you break down the door and come and get me and take me away so they wouldn't hurt me? They devoured my heart and spit it back out. There were so many boys and men, why didn't you break the door down and rescue me? If I was worth saving, then why did I feel so worthless? I never thought you or anybody loved me. Even now I don't feel loved by you. Why don't you want me? Couldn't you have made me so people would love me?"

"I chose you to be especially close to me. I'm sorry for your suffering. I suffered with you. Every time you brought your sins and tears to me repeatedly I said to you, 'I forgive you!' I forgave you then, and I forgive you now. I forgave you for all eternity, but every time you ran away from me, thinking I was going to reject you and leave you.

"Everyone you have ever loved has hurt you. You're afraid if you love me, I will leave you, too. You just don't know how much I want to be with you, precious Cindy. If you accept my forgiveness, I will open the door and come into you. Do you want me to come into you and be with you and love you for all eternity?"

"Yes, Lord, I accept your forgiveness. I know little Cindy is just as broken as I am, more broken, really. She didn't know there was a Sacred Heart who wants to love her and be close to her and protect her from the wolves. Now adult Cindy and little Cindy are one in the same. They are both forgiven of all sins."

Angels are singing. Beautiful music is playing. Candles are burning. Rainbows are in the sky, and Jesus is dancing, laughing and holding little Cindy in one arm and adult Cindy in the other. She has come home. She is safe. She is loved. She is finally loved.

— Cindy

Congratulations, Cindy!

It sounds like you had a powerful healing experience with the Lord. After my spirit-filled encounter with the Lord, I had the most euphoric week of my life. If felt so good, I thought it would last forever. Kind of like the honeymoon after a marriage. I'm still married to the Lord, and his presence dwells inside my heart, but looking back, I wish I had spent more time with him that week.

His presence was so powerful it overwhelmed me. I could hardly endure five minutes of that intensity, and then I would back away from the prayer. Looking back, I wish I had tried harder. I should have abandoned everything and submerged myself deep into his endless love.

— Rob

Chapter Sixteen

Dear Rob,

Last night I felt nothing but peace and joy. I could hardly sleep all night, thinking of him. I woke up thinking of him and had that fullness in my heart again after Holy Communion. My best friend Jamie, who was at Mass with me, said I was glowing.

My heart just wants to go off and be with the Lord. I know there's so much more that I could be experiencing. I would like to go away on retreat if I could. Maybe I can at some point, but right now my family wouldn't let me.

I love my family with all my heart. I'm so grateful for my husband, children and grandchildren. I wouldn't want to live a day without them, but I feel so controlled by everybody. I still get down about this, but I'm offering everything up to the Lord.

I'm ready to do more healing work, whenever you are. I'm still fasting, but it has been really hard lately. I'm also nervous about going off my fast next week. I don't want to slip back to that place ever again.

— Cindy

Dear Cindy,

If you want to do more healing work, I remember a scene from the Holy Land that could use a little more attention. You had to sit next to the cleric on the plane ride home after he berated you in front of everybody. Why don't you describe what happened?

In this exercise I would like to see you fight his lies with the truth. It will help you be more assertive. If you can be more assertive with the cleric, you will be able to be more assertive with your family. Send over what happened, and I will show you how to fight using the sword of the Spirit.

— Rob

Dear Rob,

It's going to be hard to remember what the cleric said, because I was in such a state of shock when he went off. I just wanted it to be over. I had to pray really hard to remember the words he used. He started screaming things like, "Who do you think you are? You are nothing! I have always shown mercy to you, but you don't show mercy to others."

I have never been mean to anybody my whole life. I don't know why he said that. It was over a disagreement with somebody in the ministry that I had months earlier. I don't know why he chose this moment to go off. The other person was actually putting Father down for something, and I was standing up for him.

I don't even remember the specific circumstances, but it involved my inability to tell him something. He was always telling me to quit running to him with every little thing, and to start making executive decisions. The one and only time I didn't go to him, and I tried to make a decision on my own, all hell broke loose.

During the yelling session, he said, "You have no right to make decisions about anything. You know nothing. You are only to do what I tell you to do. You were nobody when I found you, and you will be nobody when I leave you. You are nothing without me."

He also said, "God will never forgive you, because you don't forgive others. You mean nothing to him. You mean nothing to me. Nothing. I don't want someone like you working for me. You will always be alone, because you are a nothing."

After he said all that to me, I went into the bathroom. I thought I was going to die. I wanted to die, but I had to go back and act like nothing happen. I had to get through the evening. My friend and I were in charge of the whole surprise party. Holy Land dignitaries were going to be there.

My friend came into the bathroom and said, "You have to pretend like nothing happened, or you will ruin everything." So that's what I did. It took all the courage I had in me not to cry. I just got up, went back out, sat down beside him, and acted as if nothing happened.

He used to always berate me in private, but this was the first time he ever berated me in public. He used to tell me that he hated to say these things to me, but that was how God dealt with him, and so that was how he had to deal with me. I think this is why I became so afraid of the Lord. I didn't want him yelling at me like that, too.

— Cindy

Don't worry, Cindy.

Jesus isn't going to yell at you.

To heal this experience, I want you to ask Jesus for the full armor of God. It's a biblical requirement for all Christians. Ephesians 6:11 commands us to put it on and never take it off. After Jesus gives you the full armor, take the sword of the Spirit and go back in time to rescue young Cindy.

By using an imagination technique, I want you to take young Cindy into another room and teach her about the full armor of God. Ephesians 6: 14–17 says, *Stand therefore, and fasten the belt of truth around your waist, and put on the breast-plate of righteousness. As shoes for your feet put on whatever will make you ready to proclaim the gospel of peace. With all of these, take the shield of faith, with which you will be able to quench all the flaming arrows of the evil one. Take the helmet of salvation, and the sword of the Spirit, which is the word of God.*

I want you to help young Cindy put on the full armor of God. You already have Christ dwelling in your heart. Make sure young Cindy has invited Christ into her heart. After you both are filled with the power and presence of Christ, I want you to draw your swords and get ready for battle.

Before you walk through the door to confront the cleric, I want you to denounce the false god of other people's approval. It doesn't matter if there are dignitaries in the room. When St. Paul stood before the kings and dignitaries of the world, God required him to speak the words of truth in love.

Once you have denounced the false god of other people's approval, I want you to walk through the door and confront the cleric. Look into his angry eyes. As soon as he opens his mouth and starts screaming angry words at you, I want you to stand in the truth. I want you to say, "I bind you, spirit of anger, in the name of Jesus!" Keep saying this over and over until the angry spirit leaves him.

This is important because when the cleric is yelling at you, he is not filled with the Holy Spirit. He is filled with the demonic spirit of anger, rage and condemnation. If you accept his angry words of condemnation, you may also be accepting a demonic spirit of condemnation as well.

After you bind up all the demonic influences that may have attached themselves to you during the cleric's berating session, I want you to start destroying the cleric's lies. When he says, "Who do you think you are?" I want you to quote Scripture. Say in an assertive voice, "I'm a child of God! Jesus died on the cross for my sins. I have been bought for a price. I belong to God. I am Jesus' little lamb and Jesus loves me!"

When the cleric says, "You were nobody when I found you, and you will be nobody when I leave you," I want you to respond, "I belong to the Lord Jesus Christ of Nazareth. I'm his faithful servant. I'm required to be obedient to Jesus. The purpose of my life is to please and serve Jesus. My self-worth and value comes from Jesus, not from earthly humans."

I want you to stand up for the truth and speak the truth in love. I want you to confront all his lies and stand up for God's truth. I want you to tell him how priests are called to a higher standard. Tell him he needs to repent before it's too late. Let me know what happens next.

— Rob

Dear Rob,

I prayed all day yesterday and tried to do what you asked me to do. I started out feeling guilty and had thoughts such as, *You are exaggerating. He didn't really talk to you that way.* I had to battle these thoughts and feelings all day. I would pray, and the Lord would say, "Yes, he did."

I also wondered why I stayed for so long. I really needed to pray about the reason why. I also needed to get to a point where I could feel compassion for this man, instead of fear. Late last night, I got to that point. This morning, I'm going to Adoration and do what you asked me to do.

I think I can do it, but a part of me is still unsure. Why is that? Part of me says, *He's a priest. Isn't he supposed to know things that we don't know?* Then another part of me knows that all the hurtful things are true.

I read over what you wrote many times. I truly believe what you said is true. My battle is not against him. My battle is against evil. I can fight evil because I have the Lord inside of me. I want to see, speak and live in truth. I want to do it for the Lord, so I can get closer to him and help bring others to him.

— Cindy

Dear Cindy,

There is one more thing you may want to denounce, and that is making a priest and the Catholic Church your god. Many Catholics fall into this trap. I grew up thinking that if I did what the Church told me, then I must be in right relationship with God.

Other Catholics think if they schmooze the parish priest, it will earn them points with God. Neither the Catholic Church nor the parish priest is your god. You have only one God, and the Lord is a jealous God. He allows no false lovers before him! The job of the Catholic Church and a faithful priest is to get you connected with the real God. You need to be in right relationship with the Lord Jesus Christ.

The sin of making the Church and the priest your god is probably what is causing your conflicting thoughts. The sin of idolatry gives demons the right to interfere with your thoughts and emotions. Demons don't want you to denounce your false lovers and come into the light. Demons don't want you to acknowledge the truth because the truth sets people free.

— Rob

Dear Rob,

I came home and read your e-mail about false gods. You are right. You're so right about everything. I see that now so clearly about the Church and priests. Wow, that is enlightening. I will go back to Adoration and pray some more.

The Lord also told me that pleasing people instead of him made false gods out of everybody. I have been breaking the first and greatest Commandment for many years: thou shall have no false gods before me! Wow! I just didn't see it until the Lord showed me.

— Cindy

Dear Rob,

I answered the cleric in the way you wanted me to. I spoke everything from the heart and I believe the Word of God to be true. My favorite quote that I said to the cleric over and over was, "My self-worth has nothing to do with you and your approval of me."

Next, I looked into the cleric's eyes and bound the evil spirits and sent them into the lake of fire where they belong. Evil no longer rules that moment in my life.

— Cindy

Dear Cindy,

After reading your response, I think you need to do a little more work. The full armor of God works just like physical armor except it's spiritual. I would like to see you rework the scene, except this time with more emotion.

The first time you did some healing work on the Holy Land scene you were hiding behind Jesus. The next time, you were able to look the cleric in the eyes and say the words that I sent in a letter. Now, I want you to put on the full armor of God, take up the Sword of the Spirit and go into battle.

I would like you to keep working the scene. I want you to use the power that God has given you to put evil in its place. Bind the demons and rebuke the sinful man. As per Matthew 18: 15 and 17, *If another member of the church sins against you, go and point out the fault when the two of you are alone. If the member listens to you, you have regained that one. If the member refuses to listen to them, tell it to the church; and if the offender refuses to listen even to the church, let such a one be to you as a Gentile and a tax collector.*

Your job as a servant of Christ is to reconcile men to God. Sin separates men from God. You are not helping the sinner by looking the other way or pretending it didn't hurt or it didn't happen.

If you accept physical abuse driven by demons, you are opening yourself up to demonic oppression. The demons can enter into your mind and heart through your acceptance of that abuse. They will make you believe you deserve it, and keep you held in bondage to that abusive relationship.

As a child of God, you are required to pass along your Father's commandments. You are required to stand up for what is right. You are required to defend the poor, the widow, the neglected and the abused. You are required to put on the full armor of God and start advancing the kingdom here on earth.

— Rob

Dear Cleric,

I'm angry. I am so angry! You have already taken up so much of my valuable life, and now I've got to sit here and give you more time. I'm sick of it, and I'm sick of you! I thought I feared you, but I don't fear you. I fear what I might do if I ever saw you, because I'm so angry.

Why did you hurt me like you did? All I ever did was love you and try to help you. I believed in you. I trusted you. You cut my heart out piece by piece, and you stepped on it and kicked it and left it to bleed, until there was no life left in me. Then you took advantage of my vulnerability, and you messed with my mind until I didn't even know what truth was anymore.

How dare you! What gives you the right to do such a thing? You are supposedly a priest of God. Why do you have to hurt people? You are such a fake! You hurt people, use them and say bad things about them. You do it to everybody. Why did I think you wouldn't do it to me?

I was so blind and taken in by your charisma, which you like to brag about so much. You are a sick man. You need help and lots of it. You used to tell me women killed themselves over you. How sick is that?

You had me so brainwashed, I didn't know light from darkness anymore. And worst of all, I could have gone to hell because of you! Let me tell you something else, you're not worth it! You are a little bitty man who squirms like a snake around women.

You take the goodness of a friendship and turn it into something sick. Then you try to convince the person they wanted it. I never wanted you like that. I don't know what you did to me to make me want to dress for a priest! You knew my sins and my insecurities, and you used them against me. How dare you!

The night you held me down, you put a fear of men in me that I carry with me to this day! Even when I was almost raped as a teenager, I wasn't as scared of those drunk guys as I was of you! You scared me because you are a priest, and I was afraid of what you would do to me if I ever left you.

I almost sold my soul to the devil by believing in you. I still opened the door to him by being associated with you. How many nights have I woke up screaming because of you? I have had it! You took my heart and my mind, and you messed them up so badly, that for two years I used to cry constantly. Two years! How could you do that to another human being who trusted you?

I'm not the bad person you said I was. I don't deserve to be yelled at by anybody, because I'm God's child. Jesus loves me. He would accept you, too, if you repented. Maybe by now you have. I hope so. I have nothing more to give you, except my forgiveness, which I give you now, and my hope that you have repented and are not hurting any more innocent lambs.

I hope you have turned away from the darkness and accepted the light. I'm in the light now, and this is the last door of darkness I have to close. I will close it on you, or you can come out, and I'll close it behind you. It's your choice.

I'm closing the door, by my own free will. Not you or anybody, not even the devil, can take my free will away from me. I choose the Lord with all my being, with all my heart and with all my soul. The only person I vow to serve is Jesus Christ. He is my Master. He is the one whom I choose.

Slam! The door is shut! The sign reads: Keep out, devil!

— Cindy

Chapter Seventeen

Good work, Cindy.

I was happy to see some anger come out of you. Anger can be a very good God-given emotion, just like the time when Jesus grew angry. By failing to work through your anger, it's very easy to get trapped in victim mode.

Healing occurs by digging up all the emotions, including anger. When a person realizes their self-worth, and someone abuses them, the natural response is anger. Once you vent all the anger, then you can truly forgive the person who hurt you.

Also, congratulations on completing 39.25 days of your vegetable and water fast! The big day is just around the corner. Forty days just like Jesus in the wilderness, is a major accomplishment! You should be proud of yourself. I am very proud of you!

— Rob

Dear Rob,

I really don't want to tell you this, but if I don't bring everything into the light, I know Satan will use it against me. Please don't be mad at me. You can't be madder at me than I am at myself. I have been trying all day to get to Jesus in the Blessed Sacrament. If I could have gotten there, I think I would have done better.

I ended up eating vegetables most of the day, because I was afraid I would start eating out of control. Well, my fear was justified. I binged. Just as an alcoholic starts drinking with one drink, I started eating with one bite. I'm so ashamed.

One day off fasting, and I'm bingeing again. What's wrong with me? Once I started, I couldn't stop. I've only stopped now because I'm sick. Please don't be mad, and please don't yell at me. Please don't give up on me. I feel like Peter when he betrayed the Lord three times.

I have a family reunion I have to go to tomorrow, and I lost it. My mother called, which is always bad for me. I still have a tendency to punish myself. I can't be victorious, because I feel that I don't deserve to be victorious. That's the only way I know how to explain it. Please don't be mad at me.

— Cindy

Dear Cindy,

I'm still very proud of you. Forty days is a huge accomplishment. You are doing a great job! Now pick yourself up off the floor, put on the full armor of God and start to fight.

Here's the prayer that I want you to pray: *God, please make me hate my sin of binge eating. Please take away all the pleasure that I think I'm receiving and show me the ugliness of my actions. Make me hate my sin. Open my eyes and allow me to see everything from your perspective. Help me turn away from food. Correct me and help me turn to you. May your love be my source and strength of comfort.*

The Lord can use anything to help his children grow in holiness. Ask him to use this experience to teach you a valuable lesson. Confess your sin before him and accept his forgiveness. Don't shame yourself or beat yourself up. It will only make you feel worse and make you want to eat more.

I'm guilty of binge eating myself. There are times when my stomach's not hungry for food, but I will make popcorn or buy ice cream in an attempt to pleasure my flesh in front of the television. Afterwards, I feel twice as bad. The only way to make myself feel better is to spend time with God in prayer.

After I buy junk food, if there is anything left over the next morning, I throw it out. I don't want it in my house. I usually feel sick and lazy the following morning. My body had to work extra hard that night to remove all the chemicals, grease and junk from my system.

When I wake up in the morning, I can feel the destructive consequences. I usually feel sluggish and tired. I don't feel like working out. I'm usually mad at myself, and the first thing I do is grab the half-eaten container of ice cream and send it down the drain.

You should try it. It is very rewarding! Cookies and ice cream have a different appearance floating in the toilet. You might want to tell Satan where to go and then give it a flush. Keep repeating the words over and over again. Say them out loud if necessary:

I bind you, Satan, in the name, power and authority of Jesus Christ. Greater is he who is in me than he who is in the world. No weapon that is fashioned against me will stand. Jesus loves me, and I am his obedient little lamb.

— Rob

Dear Rob,

I'm back and ready to fight.

— Cindy

Dear Cindy,

Where do you want to start? Do you need help fighting the food addiction in the present? Where are the attacks coming from? How is your family involved? What's going on with you in regards to eating and spending time with the Lord?

— Rob

Dear Rob,

I need help fighting the food addiction in the present. I did what you said and had every intention of eating healthy today, and then all of a sudden, I did it again! I'm so mad at myself!

I really don't know why I'm doing this again, except that I have had some very uncomfortable things I've had to deal with and attend to. I don't do crowds well, and I don't do family stuff well either. I should be spending extra time with the Lord instead of bingeing.

Sometimes I binge to make myself feel better, but I also binge when I feel the need to punish myself. That's why when you say you're proud of me, you can't know how much that means to me. Nobody ever says that to me. Nobody! More than anything, I want the Lord to be proud of me, but I feel that I fail him daily.

I still have guilt when I talk about my mother. I was feeling better about my mother after I gave her to Jesus in front of the tabernacle, but all she has to do is call, and she totally messes me up again. She is such a sad and hurting human being. A part of me feels like I'm failing the Lord by not helping her in some way. I've tried to help her for 51 years, but nothing I do is ever good enough.

— Cindy

Dear Cindy,

Let's start with the food addiction. As soon as you are eating healthy, we will continue working on your assertive training techniques and deal with your mother. Let's bring your eating situation into the light. Tell me what's going on. What have you been eating, and what should you be eating? It may be helpful to plan your menu for tomorrow. What would the ideal menu look like?

— Rob

Dear Rob,

I've been eating fried chicken and German potato salad from a place that we love back home. We brought some home with us. It's pretty much gone now. I told my family to eat the rest tonight, or it's going in the toilet as you suggested.

Before, I binged on more fried food. I was thinking about chips and ice cream, my all-time favorite, but hadn't got to them yet! I also had a couple of Diet Cokes. That's what I do. Once I start, I feel I've failed the Lord and I try to punish myself for not being better and stronger for him.

I'm sitting here thinking about what I should be eating, and I'm going back to mostly vegetables, with a little protein, and maybe some fruit, with some salad dressing for salads, and decaf tea. I thought I would try kind of a semi-fast for the Lord. I drink tea all the time now. Sometimes cold, but mostly hot. I drink lots of water, too. I used to never drink water at all. How does this sound?

— Cindy

Dear Cindy,

I would like to hear more about self-punishment. How does overeating tie into self-punishment? Where did you learn this? Who taught you this concept? What kind of thoughts do you think before you punish yourself?

It will be helpful to plan your diet for tomorrow and then stick to it. I would also like to see you remove Diet Coke, ice cream and chips from your house. It would be great if you could say to your family, "Today everybody is going to start eating healthy, and junk food will no longer be allowed in this house. Because of my great love for everybody, I want us all to start eating more healthy."

What would happen if you said that to your family? Would they support you?

Let's eliminate this self-punishment issue right away. Please spend the necessary time and ask the Holy Spirit to shine his light on the topic. I want you to uncover as much information as possible.

— Rob

Chapter Eighteen

Dear Rob,

I just spent hours with the Lord bawling and journaling. I asked the Holy Spirit to help me understand why I hate myself so much and why I feel the need to punish myself, and why I think overeating fulfills that need.

If I didn't feel like the scum of the earth before, I sure do now. Going through all these painful memories doesn't do much for my self-esteem. I really don't want to share all this garbage with you either. I've already embarrassed myself to the limit, but here it goes:

I don't deserve to have a healthy body or to live a happy life, because I'm a bad person. I deserve to hurt myself and be fat and ugly so nobody will want to be with me. I deserve nothing good. I can't eat good food, because that will make me feel good, and I don't deserve any goodness. The more I eat bad, the worse I feel about myself. The worse I feel about myself, the more I think I should eat bad food to punish myself, because I'm a bad person.

I also use food to zone out and escape.

I eat large quantities of bad food, because I don't deserve to have a healthy body. I deserve to be ugly on the outside, because I'm ugly on the inside. Who told me? My mother used to always tell me this in all kinds of ways.

If anyone liked or loved me, she would get jealous. She always wanted all the attention. She never wanted me to have any. Every day I got constant criticism and rejection from her. The cleric did the same thing. A part of me knew that he would never have anything to do with me if I was fat. They both demanded perfection from me, but I failed them both. It was like walking on eggshells with constant berating.

My mother always told me I was the black sheep. I was always trying to earn my mother's love, but I never could. My mom always said I was fake and that if anyone got to know the real me, they would see the truth and leave me. I know my mother has never felt loved her whole life. She made sure I never would either.

After the eighth grade, I went into the convent to be a nun. I got homesick the first night and soon came back home. When I walked in the door, my mom said, "I told you you're a bad seed. Now God knows, too." From that day forward, I believed God was mad at me and that I really was a bad seed. I felt like a black sheep and a reject for all eternity.

I didn't deserve to go to heaven anymore. I went home a failure, stupid and inept. After I had disappointed God, I decided I didn't deserve to be happy, healthy or holy. I started hanging around with the wrong crowd, because I wanted to be with my own kind. After that, I really went downhill.

Somewhere in my childhood I got the idea that the only way I could be close to God was to be a nun. By leaving the convent, I committed the worst sin ever. God could never love me after that, because I went home a failure. If I ever forgot it for a second, my mother would remind me.

The cleric just picked up where my mother left off. For some reason I thought if I stayed with him, God would love me. I thought he had a special connection with God. I stayed with him because I was also trying to earn God's love back.

I've always tried to help others be closer to God. I know God is wonderful. It's like God's in this big beautiful room. I know he's in there, so I go out and find hurting people and I open the door and put them inside the room so God can love them and comfort them. I want to go in the room, too, but I know I can't.

I'm like Moses. I screwed up. I can never see the Promised Land. I can never feel God's touch. I can only love him from a distance and help others love him. I always try to bring others to him. I know he's wonderful. I want them to have the joy, peace and love only he can give.

What is my thought right before I eat? *You are no good. God doesn't love you. How could he? How could anybody? You do not deserve to be happy. You must look like you are — ugly. You are a nothing. Fat people are invisible, and that's what you deserve to be.*

As I'm sitting here writing this, I'm thinking I don't deserve to live. I'm too messed up. The world would be better off without me. If I had a bottle of pills, I would take them, except I'm too afraid I would go to hell, and I don't want to go to hell. I don't want to hurt my family and I don't want to hurt Jesus. The pain runs so deep…

How much longer can I go on living these lies? I'm so afraid. I want to be a child of God and be loved by him, but I'm afraid if I go in the room, he will say, *Get out! You aren't holy enough to be in here with me. Go out and live with the other black sheep.*

If I'm not punishing myself by overeating, then that means I deserve to go in the room with the Lord and be happy, healthy and holy, but I can't go in because I'm undeserving. If I did go in, he would just tell me to leave. It's better to stay out here and punish myself than to go in the room and have God punish me. I couldn't bear to hear him say, *You have to leave.* My heart would break in two.

At least this way I can be with him from a distance. I peek in the window often. I know he's wonderful, and I know that all the people I take to the room go in and are happy and get what they need. Maybe someday I'll be able to go into the room, too.

— Cindy

Dear Rob,

Please disregard the letter I sent to you last night. I was in a really dark place.

I sat alone in church tonight, just the Lord and me. The staff just locks me in now, and I go out a special door that locks by itself. I stayed with him into the night. I didn't want to leave. I just sat and cried and cried, and I felt he cried with me. I feel better getting all that garbage out of me the other night, but I'm totally embarrassed and ashamed. Please just disregard!

— Cindy

Dear Cindy,

It looks like you made a brilliant discovery. Little Cindy was abused by her mom and starved for love. Now it is time to go back into your past and give little Cindy the love that she deserves. It will also help to give big Cindy the love that she deserves. There are two ways to do this:

The first is to go back in time using an imagination technique and revisit little Cindy. You will need to go back in time with Jesus and play with little Cindy. Take some presents for her. Make sure they are wrapped in brightly colored paper, and go back with me for a surprise party. Tell her we are here from her future because we love her.

She's a beautiful little girl who tries so hard to please everybody. Tell her she is precious and that we love her so much. Tell her we bought her lots of presents and that we are going to spend the whole day in her honor. Tell her we can do anything she wants. Just ask her where she would like to go.

If little Cindy wants to go to the zoo, then we will go to the zoo, and she can see all the animals she wants. She can ask all the questions she wants, and no one will shame her. We will let her lead the way and spend all the time she wants at the zoo.

If little Cindy wants to go shopping at a store, then we will go to the store, and she can buy anything she wants. She can also touch anything she wants, and no one will yell at her. I have a special surprise to give her, a credit card that she can use to buy herself new clothes. I want to go clothes shopping, and afterwards, I want to go toy shopping. Big Cindy and Jesus can help by telling little Cindy what clothes look the coolest. She is a very beautiful little girl, and I want you to fix her hair and pick out all the best clothes.

After we go shopping, let's stop by the spa. Maybe little Cindy would like to have her nails done. I have a feeling Jesus wants to buy little Cindy some jewelry. Afterwards we can go play and then go to the amusement park. Wherever little Cindy wants.

I want big Cindy to spend the next week loving little Cindy. I want big Cindy to speak all the loving words that little Cindy needs to hear. I want big Cindy to spend all week loving, praying with, listening to and caring about little Cindy.

The second part of this exercise is for big Cindy to practice her affirmations. Do you remember when we first started working together and I asked you to write 50 positive statements about yourself? For some reason you were only able to write five. Here's the five you wrote along with the others I promised you:

I'm a servant of the Lord.
I want God's will in my life.
I'm a loving wife and mother.
I'm a Catholic saint.
I'm a child of the light.
I'm a woman of great strength.
I'm a woman of great courage.
I'm a woman of great beauty.
God created me to be beautiful.
God created me to be healthy and holy.
God created me to be free.
I deserve to be healthy.
I deserve to eat good foods.
I deserve to be loved.

I have the right to make mistakes.
I have the right to express my true feelings.
I am real, and my friends love me.
I am Jesus' little white lamb.
Jesus loves me.

I want you to add ten more positive affirmations to this list and say them out loud every day from here on out. These loving affirmations will help you love yourself and see yourself as Jesus sees you. They will overpower all the lies the enemy taught you through your mom's abuse. Jesus says the truth sets people free. I want you to affirm the positive truth about yourself every day in the morning when you get up.

Please share with me all the fun places that little Cindy wants to go. It would be great if you could send over a different adventure every day.

— Rob

Dear Rob,

Today has been great. I can't tell you how much the positive affirmations are helping. Every time I start to have bad thoughts, I read them, and it really helps. I also added ten more to the list you gave me.

I'm loyal.
I'm trustworthy.
I'm compassionate.
I'm forgiving.
I have a right to my privacy.
I have a right to make my own decisions.
I have a right to spend time with Jesus.
I have a right to feed my soul.
I have a right to exercise my body.
I have a right to feel good about myself.

They have helped me so much. I have eaten healthy at every meal. I didn't want to binge once, not at all!

I feel so much better getting all that garbage out of me the other night. I feel a little bad for what I said about my mother, but I keep hearing the Lord say, "It's true. You still love her and have forgiven her, but you had to bring it to the light."

A huge weight has been lifted off of me.

Guess what? You, Jesus, little Cindy and I have been at the beach all day! It has been really fun! I only got to see the ocean once, but I love it. Today we have been playing in the ocean and walking in the sand. We all hold hands. It's a secluded, private beach with incredible white sand so that we can walk barefoot and feel the sand between our toes.

There was a light breeze and beautiful seagulls flying over the water, and dolphins. It's really peaceful and beautiful. I was glowing all day thinking about it. It felt so good to be there with you, Jesus and little Cindy. It was good to see her laugh. I don't remember her laughing much before. She wasn't afraid at all. It was so good to see her not afraid. When she's not afraid, I don't feel afraid.

I know the fasting isn't about weight loss, but I have lost 20 pounds so far!

You won't believe what else happened today. I tried to join a fitness center. I couldn't wait to come home and tell you. I said tried because my family and friends threw a fit. They are insisting I see a doctor first because of all my health issues. That's how good I feel today. I want to get healthy. I feel that it's OK to try to get healthy.

Several things came up with my family again. They love me, and I love them with all my heart, but they all seem to take their bad moods out on me. They all try to control me. They also make me feel like I have to get their approval on everything.

After reading the affirmations today, I decided that the only person I had to get approval from was the Lord. He and I had a great day! I feel there is a lot of light pouring into me and there's room for more light to come in me, because the darkness is coming out. It's really cool. Several times today it brought me to tears just thinking about it. I feel so much lighter.

Even though I had some bad moments, I was able to take them to the Lord and not abuse myself with food. Last night, I had to fight and fight not to binge, but I didn't! I made it through the night. The Lord honored my efforts last night and made it easier today. I have hardly eaten anything today, and I could care less.

I was too busy being with him. I don't think I've ever felt so peaceful. I know now why God gave me such a good imagination. I prayed and played with little Cindy on and off all day. She enjoyed it so much. I'm crying again. It makes me cry to hear her laugh. It makes me cry to feel safe. It makes me cry to think this is what the Lord wants for me. It makes me cry that I'm really getting to know him. I think I'm really starting to be able to open myself up to him and let him come into me. It's so great! Thank you so much for everything!

— Cindy

Dear Cindy,

You are making tremendous progress. I'm very proud of you. Keep up the good work. Keep doing what you have been doing. Keep saying your affirmations. Keep spending time with the Lord and please keep loving little Cindy.

Let me know if little Cindy would like to feed the seagulls. It's very fun. When there's a breeze, the birds can hover in midair and catch bread in flight. It's fun to pick which bird you want to get the next piece of bread and then watch them catch it.

Has little Cindy ever been to the boardwalk? There are all kinds of rides and fun events right around the corner...

— Rob

Dear Rob,

I thought we would go to the beach today in Hawaii. I always thought it would be beautiful and guess what, it's incredible. Every morning the Lord creates a sunrise like a new painting of brightly colored love for us to enjoy. He literally brings his light into the darkness and illuminates the sky in a thousand different shades of exquisite beauty. That is how my soul is starting to feel. As the Lord's light is coming in, the darkness is going away.

This morning everyone gathered flowers and we made leis to wear around our necks. We tried to get Jesus to buy a Hawaiian shirt, but he wouldn't. He's just a basic white robe and sandals kind of guy. I love watching his hair blow in the wind. His face is so kind. He's always smiling at me. He never gets mad at me for anything. He even carried little Cindy on his shoulders today.

We built sand castles, and then Jesus let us cover him with sand. He even laughed out loud about it. I love hearing little Cindy laugh. I really love hearing Jesus laugh. His laugh just melts you. Then we all lay down and looked up at the clouds and took turns describing what we were seeing. We all looked at the same clouds, but we all saw different things in them.

Jesus teased us that his interpretation was the correct one because his Daddy drew it. We just started laughing and laughed all day. It's so fun being together with the three of you. Little Cindy is really enjoying everything. She doesn't get too close to Jesus yet, but he will walk over and take her hand. She loves it when he does that.

At one point, little Cindy took a pail of water and splashed

Jesus. He thought that was so funny and didn't get mad or anything. Everything little Cindy does seems to delight him wholeheartedly. I cry to see the love he has for her and for you. I'm not feeling his love so much today, but that's OK. I'm grateful to just be in his presence with all of you.

Watching the sun go down on the beach tonight was breathtaking. The wind was blowing through the palm trees, the seagulls were resting and the water was rushing up against the rocks. Everything was settling down for the night to go to sleep.

Sleeping with Jesus in your midst is very comforting. It's like when the Apostles were in the boat during the storm. Jesus just slept through it. When you're with him, you know you will get through the storm, too. He won't let anything bad happen to you. I wish I could be with him like this always.

— Cindy

Chapter Nineteen

Dear Rob,

Today, Jesus bought out a whole movie theater just for us. I always wanted to go to the movies as a child, but my parents hardly ever took me.

We watched some really good classics. Jesus knows all the good movies. Little Cindy got to sit on Jesus' lap. She really likes the personal attention that he's been showing her. Touching Jesus and being held by him is the greatest thing. We also ate some special popcorn that Jesus made for us. It was air-popped and healthy.

Tonight we're going to a drive-in movie. We're going to lie on blankets and watch the movie under the stars. I don't know what's going to be showing. Jesus wants to surprise everybody. He says he wants to spend a lot more time like this with me and little Cindy. He doesn't want us letting others take away our joy all the time like they do.

We talked to our mother today, and some other bad things happened, and adult Cindy started bingeing again. She is really sorry. Little Cindy told her not to cry. We just talked all this over with Jesus, and he told us to tell you, but not to dwell on it. He has forgiven her again for everything, and we are going to go play and pray some more and be happy.

I can't wait to see what movie the Lord has picked out for us to see. It's a beautiful night, and there are so many brightly shining stars. Jesus is so much fun to hang out with. He is so loving and forgiving. He wipes your tears away and hugs you tight. He looks you in the eye, and he never looks past you. I can see Jesus so clearly these days. I see him in my mind's eye, and I feel him in my heart. It's the best feeling.

I'm back now, in this moment with him, in him and through him. We are going to love little Cindy some more and laugh and talk into the night.

— Cindy

Dear Cindy,

I wish everybody could have such a beautiful and trusting relationship with the Lord as you do. I'm so happy for you. The devil has been using fear all your life to keep you away from the Lord's love.

I'm so happy you and the Lord are developing a passionate and intimate relationship. If I were you, I would take advantage of this sacred honeymoon reunion and spend as much time as possible communing with the lover of your soul.

— Rob

Dear Rob,

I didn't want to tell you this, but the Lord has been convicting me about something. I was trying my best to ride it out and see if it went away. This morning I had a breakthrough on an issue that I have been fighting my whole life — letting people and circumstances make me sad.

I don't think the Lord wants me to do that anymore. He wants me to keep my focus on him and our relationship. I'm not God, and I cannot change people or the events in their lives. I can only pray for them and surrender everything to the Lord.

I don't know if this makes any sense to you, or if you understand what I'm talking about. It makes perfect sense to me. I have to get out of self-pity mode completely. It's not easy to admit, but I'm admitting. I also have to realize that all can be used for good if I turn it over to the Lord. I just wanted to share that with you.

— Cindy

Dear Rob,

I have had the worst attacks since about Saturday afternoon. I haven't been able to have any more fun times with little Cindy. I've tried, but they won't come. The affirmations seem like lies to me now. I would like to say I didn't binge, but I would be lying. I started to e-mail you several times, but I wanted to work it out with the Lord first.

I started feeling bad about myself, feeling that there was no hope for me. I know the Lord doesn't want me to let people take away my joy, and I'm trying, but when you get run over by a Mack truck, you're going to bleed. I can't control the people and circumstances around me, so I get depressed, and that's when I want to punish myself with food.

Satan has been whispering filth in my ear about what a bad person I am. I believed him at first, and I was going to e-mail you and tell you it's over. I'll never change. There's no hope for me. But like I told you, I want to fight for the Lord more than I hate myself. I kept praying and journaling and playing praise music and going to church.

I know it's only been a couple of days, but it feels like an eternity. I cried a lot of tears and fought a lot of battles. I lost with the food, but I won with prayer and turning to Jesus. I think that's good, don't you?

Maybe this is what you mean by putting on the armor of God. I still keep doing what God wanted, even though I don't feel it. I just don't know how to stop bingeing. I don't want Satan to have this stronghold on me. Maybe I need to go back to fasting. I'll do whatever you tell me to do. Please don't be mad at me.

— Cindy

Dear Cindy,

You need to get up off the ground and fight. There's a lot riding on you. The Lord has big plans for you. There's a lot of people out there who need you. Now get up! Rise to your feet, mighty soldier, Cindy!

Rule number one — fighting is not about feelings. It doesn't matter if you don't feel like practicing your affirmations or not, you need to do them regardless of your feelings. Do them a hundred times a day until the feelings start to follow.

Do you remember the story in my book about when my boat sank? I was out in the dark, in the rain, waist deep in a lake, trying to rescue my personal property from the hull of my capsized boat. I didn't feel like praising God, but I did it anyhow. I started praising God and eventually my feelings started to follow.

You have a major calling on your life, and I can guarantee you, you will be tested. Satan demanded to sift Peter like wheat, and I'm sure he will put you to the test as well. All you need to do is stand strong. Pass the test. Fight for victory. If you resist the devil, he will flee from you.

Rule number two — keep the finish line in sight. You need a goal in life, a purpose, a passion to fight for, something to keep your focus directed, a pursuit to keep you striving towards victory.

Rule number three — there is no such thing as quitting. The Lord will never give up on you. He will never, ever, give up on you. You only have one option: stand your ground and fight.

We need to address your family's dynamics. You have e-mailed me several times concerning this, and now it is time to get back to assertiveness training. I have the feeling they treat you like an emotional punching bag. Whenever someone has a bad day, they look for Cindy to vent their frustration on.

Send over some examples. You said a few days ago the Lord was convicting you about something. Tell me what's going on. We need to put an end to all the unhealthy behavior in your life and household once and for all.

I can't reiterate this point enough — the Lord has big plans for you, and you need to get up off the ground, get serious, focused and disciplined and ready to fight. There are a lot of people out there who need you. Get up, soldier, get up now and fight!

— Rob

Dear Rob,

I'm ready to fight. I have been. I haven't binged today, and usually by this time of day, I could have caused a lot of damage. I've already gained back five pounds of the 20 I lost. It's extremely upsetting, but that's not what I'm most upset about.

I love my family more than life itself, but they have no clue how they make me feel, and I promise you, I have conditioned them to do what they do. They are all good and loving people, but they do exactly what you said. They pretty much take out their bad moods on me. Everyone acts as though my time isn't important and as if I'm not important either.

I have had to fight so hard to be able to keep going to Mass and make Holy Hours every day. It's not because they don't want me to spend time with the Lord. They just don't want it to interfere with what they want me to do for them. I've been at everybody's beck and call all my life, pleasing everybody. That's what I do. If I sneeze and they look at me wrong, I try to sneeze differently.

I've conditioned people to treat me this way. I'm always trying to get affirmation and approval from everybody, because my self-worth depends on it. That's where the Lord has been convicting me. I don't think he wants me to live like this anymore. I think he wants me to live my life more for him.

Things are totally out of order right now. I have thought so for a long time. I have to quit letting people rob me of the joy the Lord wants to give to me. For example, when someone says something to me that's not very nice, I take it into me. I internalize it and believe their words and moods are my fault, and what they are saying is true.

I pretty much try to stay out of everybody's way and not get in trouble. After they hurt me deeply and leave, I eat. I think I deserve to suffer because I failed everybody, especially if I think I failed the Lord, too. I feel as though I fail him if I don't do everything perfectly. That's when I punish myself with food.

A part of it is to escape pain, but I would say, more to punish — to punish myself for not being perfect. When I can't be perfect, it means I can't be loved. When I don't feel loved, I want to eat.

The more I listen to suffering souls who have addiction problems, the more I hear the same pain. I know how they feel. I just don't know how to help them not feel that way. I don't know how to not feel this way myself.

— Cindy

Dear Cindy,

Let's take an in-depth look at what's going on. After we bring the spiritual dynamics into the light, we can talk about your options. I know I'm treading on sensitive ground, so I will describe all this in the third-person point of view. Please let me know if it's an accurate representation of the truth.

A woman loves her family more than life itself. She lives to serve her family. She loves her family with all her heart, with all her time and with all her attention. She is at their beck and call 24/7. Whatever they want her to do, she does it, all in an attempt to make her family happy.

When the oldest son has a bad day at school, he comes home and takes his frustration out on his mom. He says, "Why didn't you do my laundry last night? It's all your fault that I had a bad day at school. If you had washed my favorite shirt, none of this would have happened!"

In the spirit realm, when the young man is displaying negative behavior, a spirit of disrespect, selfishness and anger is driving him. When he takes his frustrations out on his mom, he is not filled with the gifts of the Holy Spirit. There is a different kind of evil spirit at work that is driving his unhealthy behaviors.

When the young man focuses his anger on his mom, she instantly opens up her soul and says, "Come into me, evil spirit of anger, rage, hate, disrespect and selfishness. Bring along all your other friends, too. I hereby open up my heart and soul for you. Come into me and make me hate myself. Drive me to do all kinds of sick, self-punishing behaviors."

The young man doesn't have any reason to make changes.

He knows he can make his mom do anything he wants. He can sense her walk-on-eggshells weakness. All he has to do is show his mom contempt for her actions, and she will instantly bow down and serve him as if he were her god. All he has to do is show his disapproval, and his mom will do anything he wants. He has complete control over his mom, and he has no reason to make changes, learn healthy relationship skills or grow in holiness.

I'm sorry if this doesn't represent the truth. If I'm wrong please tell me. It will also be helpful if you could send over a detailed description the next time a conflict occurs. Please write down the words spoken and the circumstances surrounding the events.

— Rob

Dear Rob,

I don't know how you know stuff, but you got it exactly right. I mean exactly.

I want to give you another example of what happened this morning before I went to Mass. My husband is a good man. He has done and will continue to do much good in our community for so many. My children are really good, too. I'm proud of them all, and I love them all with all my heart, so when I say these things it makes me feel bad.

My husband walks into the kitchen when I'm about to leave for Mass. He and my son had slept in a little this morning. I say good morning and I start to talk to him, and he just walks away when I'm talking and goes over and turns on the TV. It's like I'm not even there. We didn't fight or have words, but these kinds of things make me feel really bad.

When I go to tell my son good-bye, he says, "Where are you going?" I say to Mass. He says, "Oh, like you're leaving us again?" I turn around to go talk to my husband again, and he won't even talk to me. I have been going to morning Mass for quite some time now. Why they have to try to make me feel guilty about it this morning, I don't know.

The good news is, I did not take it in. Aren't you proud of me? Do you know why? I recognize now that this is not coming from them. I know it's the darkness working through them. Before I thought I was fighting my family, and somehow, in my mixed-up mind, I thought I deserved to be treated like this, because I don't feel that I'm a good wife and mother for a thousand reasons.

I have a new strength seeing it this way. I will keep fighting evil for God, for my family and myself. The darkness will not win. I'm not bingeing. I didn't binge yesterday, and I haven't today either. I'm ready to do whatever I need to do. You just tell me, and I'll do it. I'm a soldier for Christ now. I have never felt stronger about it in my life. There will be no more letting the devil get me down. I know he'll attack, but from here on out, I'm fighting back! No more bingeing!

I am a soldier for Christ! I may be a torn-up soldier, but a soldier nonetheless. I'm so grateful to be a soldier for Christ!

— Cindy

Chapter Twenty

Dear Cindy,

There are several ways a soldier of Christ can fight this battle: you have already won the majority of the victory by not taking it personally. Once you own enough internal strength and self-worth, all you need to do is ask a few questions and help your family be more loving.

For example, let's say your husband made a critical remark like, "The dress you are wearing is ugly." Instead of allowing this comment to ruin your day and cause self-punishing behaviors, all you need to do is ask him why he said it.

He would probably respond, "Because the dress is ugly, it's bright orange, and it makes you look terrible."

After you have created a conversation, you can help your husband be more loving. Ask yourself, *What should my husband be saying?* Maybe you could help him rephrase the statement and see if he agrees. You could say something like, "It sounds like you want me to look my best for our dinner date. Is there another dress you like better?"

Your husband might say, "Yes, you look better in the black dress."

You reply, "So what you are saying is that because you love me and want me to look my best, you would rather see me wear the black dress instead of the orange dress. Is that correct?"

Another example comes from the morning Mass incident. Your son says, "Where are you going?"

Your response would be, "To morning Mass."

Your son: "Oh, like you are leaving us again."

To create a conversation, I would ask the simple question, "Why are you saying this to me?" Maybe he feels abandoned. Maybe he's trying to shame you for going to church. Your job is not to take it personally, just create a healthy conversation. I would say, "Yes, I'm going to Mass because I need the power of God to help me fight my food addiction. No, I'm not abandoning you. I love you, and I want you to come to Mass with me. Let's all go to Mass together. Tomorrow, I will wake you up early, and we can go to Mass together."

Another technique is the *I feel* statement. Whenever your family does something disrespectful, you can say, "I feel hurt when you do that. I feel disrespected when you walk away when I'm talking to you. I feel hurt when you yell at me like that."

No one can argue with your feelings. You have the right to feel any way you want to. Instead of taking negative behavior personally and punishing yourself afterwards, the *I feel* statement brings the offense into the light. It gives the guilty party the opportunity to see their disrespectful behaviors and change their ways. By suffering abuse and keeping silent, you are enabling your family's sinful behavior and robbing them of the opportunity to be more loving.

Another weapon a soldier of Christ is required to use is the power of the Holy Spirit. It's the Holy Spirit's job to convict sinners of their sin. It is not your responsibility to try to change you husband's behavior. You will never be able to change another person's behavior because God gave everyone free will. All you need to do is call down the power of the Holy Spirit when a sinner is committing the sin.

For example, when your husband is acting in a disrespectful manner, all you need to do is invoke the power of the Holy Spirit. Say to yourself, "Come Holy Spirit." Say it silently a thousand times. "Come, Holy Spirit and help my family be more loving."

You can also bind the demonic influence and take authority over your life, house, husband, family and relationships. Just say the words silently and call upon the power of the Holy Spirit to convict the sinner of their sins. You will need to bind the demonic and call upon the Holy Spirit in the heat of the battle. Do it during the most intense moment or right before the attack breaks out.

Practice these techniques fervently for a few months, and you will see dramatic results.

— Rob

Dear Rob,

I'm still standing strong. I can't tell you how much I wanted to binge, but I haven't. The desire I'm feeling is more for comfort than punishment. I refuse to take comfort in food. Not that food really comforted me anyway. It was only a lie from the devil. When you feel sad, dark and scared, you'll grab anything. Now I want to grab the great lover of my soul.

I also wanted to tell you that your techniques are really working. My son and I had the best conversation last night. My husband is responding, too.

I'm counting the days like I did when fasting. I'm not bingeing for 40 days. I'm on day six. I'm not thinking about food as much anymore. Every time I resist the devil, and he is fleeing. This is amazing to me. The Lord has really given me strength. I could never do this before.

— Cindy

Dear Rob,

I just wanted to let you know they are admitting me to the hospital. They think I have a blood clot in my leg. I'm standing strong. Don't be worried.

— Cindy

Dear Rob,

I'm home and have been really out of it. They had me on morphine the whole time I was in the hospital. They were trying to get inflammation and swelling down.

My husband told me I can't drive while I'm on these medications. How am I going to get to Mass and Holy Hours? I'll never make it without Jesus!

To make matters worse, I just found out my mother is coming to stay for a couple days. She was mean to me on the phone, and she hasn't even gotten here yet. I already had a horrible fight with her because I asked if she'd take me to Mass tomorrow, and she refused.

I just don't know if I can handle this. I put up with her because my dad really wants to see his kids and grandkids. I'm about to lose it big-time. I need some serious prayer support. When I hung up the phone, I called her cuss words. I usually don't talk that way, but that's what she does to me.

I tried to pray all night and decided that if this is the cross the Lord is giving me, I need to pick it up like a soldier for Christ and carry it. I'm going to do better. It will be harder for me to get to Mass, and I may not be able to make Holy Hours, but I'll figure out some way to get through this.

I shouldn't give up so easily. It's just that I know how much I need the Lord in Holy Eucharist. I'm barely hanging on by a thread but I will do better from this minute forward. I will not binge. I'll get my affirmations and read them over and over before my mother gets here.

I feel bad for feeling this way. I know God loves her. I love her, too, but she hurts me deeply. I know it's because she hurts so much herself. All she knows is pain and how to inflict it on others.

— Cindy

Dear Rob,

I was feeling really bad for what I said about my mother. She brings out the worst in me. After she got here, it was worse than usual. I tried to do the new technique you taught me. I did it all day and all night with her.

When she first got here, she said some pretty terrible things. She just went on and on, endlessly. I'm listening and trying with all my might not to internalize what she is saying. At the same time, I'm leaning on the Lord as I have never leaned on him before.

Talk about surrendering. If I didn't lean on him, I would have died on the spot. I could hardly breathe. I just kept him close, and guess what? Somehow during this time, good overcame evil. I was standing in the gap between good and evil, for my family and for my mother.

Is that not the coolest thing? I'm 51 years old, and I feel like a child. It's like someone released me from an orphanage. I feel complete love for everybody on the face of the earth, love for everyone who has ever hurt me.

The fact that I'm not bingeing, under the circumstances of my mother's visit, my close friend's funeral, the hospital visit and numerous other things, is nothing short of a miracle. I have cried out for help for the longest time. I thought the Lord wasn't listening to me. I now know he heard my cry and was waiting for me to pick up my cross and follow him.

— Cindy

Dear Cindy,

I'm concerned about your examples of the cross that we all must carry. The theology of the cross can be twisted around and distorted. For example, Satan attacks a man with disease and gives the man the bright idea that it's his cross to carry. Satan is killing the man with a slow and painful death, and the man thinks he is doing God a favor by suffering.

Do you see the depravity in this kind of thinking?

God is a god of love, power and healing. There's a spiritual battle going on, and the Lord wants the man to invite his power into his life and heart to fight for victory. If the man thinks sickness is his cross, then what motivation does he have to fight for victory?

Another example comes from an overweight woman. She thought that being overweight was how the Lord created her and that it was her cross to carry. The Lord is a God of beauty, wholeness and goodness. Being overweight was not her cross to carry. In her case, overeating was a sin called licentiousness and gluttony. Instead of running to the Lord for comfort, she was running to food for comfort.

The cross is an instrument of death. We are called to put our fleshly desires to death. We are called to put our sinful nature to death, not use the doctrine of the cross to enable our sickness and disease.

In an earlier letter you mentioned your mom's visit as your cross to carry. Will you please explain this concept to me? You say you love her, yet in the same sentence you say she is a woman of great darkness. Do you feel obligated to love her? Do you feel obligated to suffer her sickness?

I want you to stop suffering other people's sickness!

— Rob

Dear Rob,

You never fail to amaze me. Oh my gosh! I never saw the cross as coming from Satan! I totally believe you and understand what you're saying. I'm happy to hear it! This definitely changes everything. The real concept of carrying the cross is putting your fleshly desires to death. I totally get it.

I feel obligated to love my mother because she's my mother. I feel bad because I try to love her and every time I have bad feelings and experience all kinds of bad fruit from being in contact with her. That's why I've considered her my cross to bear.

She causes me tremendous pain, and I thought I should put up with it because she's my mother. As I'm writing this to you, I see how this has nothing to do with the Fourth Commandment. There is nothing holy about sharing sickness that is not of the Lord. Why couldn't I see this before?

Dying to self, by putting my fleshly desires to death, is hard enough without trying to add emotional abuse from others. Just knowing it's not from the Lord releases me. I only want to do his will. No wonder there wasn't any good fruit after 51 years of trying to please my mother — it wasn't of the Lord! That alone gives me peace and hope.

— Thanks again, Cindy

Dear Rob,

I fell down under the weight of my mother's criticism the other day. I'm back up now, and I'm starting the 40 days of no bingeing over. I will try harder to make it this time. Thank you for your support.

— Cindy

Chapter Twenty-One

Dear Cindy,

After I tell you the Lord has big plans for your life, the first thing that happens is evil pounces on you, you wind up in the hospital, they dope you up on drugs so that you can't make Mass, and then your mother swoops in for the kill. She probably vomited negativity and condemnation on you all weekend. When do you plan to start the 40 days over?

— Rob

Dear Rob,

Everything you said was the truth. I started the 40 days yesterday, and by the grace of God and everything you have taught me, I'm fighting back. Being back at Mass is exactly what I needed. I haven't made a Holy Hour for about ten days, but I'm getting ready to go there in just a few minutes.

They had me on pain pills and muscle relaxers, but I'm only taking a half dose so I can drive to church. The doctors said I have bone chips in my leg from arthritis, which has caused inflammation. They are trying to get the swelling down. At first, they thought it was a blood clot, because my right leg is swollen two inches larger than my left in places.

I don't even know where to start with my mom. She totally messes with my mind and heart. She brings out all kinds of negativity in me, especially guilt. Guilt about everything. I love her, but I don't like her very much, and that makes me feel bad.

She never has a nice thing to say to me. She has never been a mother to me, or a grandmother to my children. Her condition is very sad. My old spiritual director told me to spend as little time with her as possible.

The weekend messed with me pretty bad, but not as bad as usual. I know I'm stronger now. I'm so grateful for that. Ever since you suggested I start fasting, my spirit-woman has started living. She had been dead a long time. I was dying a slow and painful death. Now I'm living with the Lord in my heart and his armor all around me. If I mess up, he pulls me back. I'm so grateful to have that kind of relationship with him now.

— Cindy

Dear Cindy,

I would like you to study 2 Corinthians 6: 14–18 in regards to your relationship with your mother: *For what partnership is there between righteousness and lawlessness? Or what fellowship is there between light and darkness? What agreement does Christ have with Beliar? Or what does a believer share with an unbeliever? What agreement has the temple of God with idols?*

For we are the temple of the living God; as God said, "I will live in them and walk among them, and I will be their God, and they shall be my people. Therefore come out from them, and be separate from them, says the Lord, and touch nothing unclean; then I will welcome you, and I will be your father, and you shall be my sons and daughters, says the Lord Almighty."

Why do you feel obligated to help your mother? Does she want your help? Are you throwing your pearls before swine in your attempts to help her? Do you feel obligated to love your mother because of society's expectations?

Is it possible to love your mother from a spiritual perspective without suffering her abuse? Is it possible to honor your mother without allowing her to verbally abuse you with shame and negativity?

Why do you think you are helping your mother? The woman comes into your house, treats you like dirt, dumps all her demonically infested negativity on you, and you open up your soul and eat every bit. Please explain how this is helping you or your mother from a spiritual perspective.

— Rob

Dear Rob,

I have read the scripture over and over. It's very hard for me to think of my mother in this light. God gave us our mothers and fathers. I don't know why, but I have a hard time connecting this scripture to my parents.

It doesn't say whom it applies to, so I guess it applies to everybody. It just doesn't feel right to walk away from a parent, because God gave us our parents. Although I can see why it's not possible to stay clean if you're wallowing in the mud.

I used to think I was helping her from a spiritual perspective, but now I see I haven't been. Allowing evil to flourish in any way can never be of the Lord. I get it now. What I have been doing is not of the Lord.

I cannot shake hands with the devil, in any way. I cannot be around fire and not get burned. I also cannot be lukewarm. I either choose life, and the Lord, or I choose death and the devil. There is no in between.

— Cindy

Dear Cindy,

There are two issues with your parents that I would like you to look at. The first issue is your need to minister to your mother. The second issue is breaking unhealthy soul-ties with your mother.

I asked you this question before — does your mom want to grow closer to God? Regardless of your mother's desire to seek God, you are probably not the person that is being called to minister to her. Before you can effectively minister to your mother, you will need to get yourself holy and healthy. You will need to break all unhealthy soul-ties and surrender your mom into the Lord's hands. You will also need to break all the unhealthy ties that keep you from acting assertively and from rejecting her abuse.

Can you look your mom in the eyes and ask her about her relationship with Jesus? Can you say, *Unless you surrender your heart and soul and bow down and serve Jesus, you run the risk of eternal separation from God?* Can you say this to your mom? If not, you are not in a position to minister to your mom. If you are not in a place called by God and anointed by God to minister to your mom, then stop trying. You are probably causing more damage than good.

It sounds like you need to break all unhealthy soul-ties with your mom. Soul-ties are all the hidden heart buttons that your mom can push, all the invisible strings that keep your soul enmeshed with hers. You gave your mom to the Lord once before and felt a little better; now it's time to break your unhealthy parent-child relationship. You are no longer mommy's little girl; you are 51 years old. Your mom has no right to treat you like a child and dump her guilt, shame and demonic filth on you. You are called to be a soldier for Christ.

A soldier for Christ has only one Master. If Christ is calling you to deliver the Gospel message to your mom, then you need to deliver it with all boldness, love and truth. Right now, you are not in a place to be able to minister to your mother, so please stop using it as an excuse to accept more of her abuse. When you are in a more assertive place, let's talk about ministering to your mother. I have all kinds of techniques that you can use to help her.

My advice is to ask the Lord to disclose all unhealthy soul-ties and agreements of enmeshment that you have with your mom and break them. This may take some time. Let me know how it goes.

— Rob

Dear Rob,

To answer your question, no, I don't think my mother wants to be holy. When I try to help her she says, "Oh no, you're the holy one. That's not for the rest of us."

I want my mom to accept the Lord's love, but it's not my decision to make. I need to worry about getting myself holy first. Even if she wants help, you're right; she is not asking for or wanting that kind of help from me. The Lord is not asking me to give that kind of help to her either.

I will keep praying for the Lord to show me all unhealthy soul-ties and agreements of enmeshment with her and ask them to be broken. You are right. She belongs to God, not to me. Her relationship with God is sacred, and I'm not the savior of her world. I see that now.

I really do think I gave her to the Lord in front of the tabernacle that night, but somehow I must have taken her back, or she just came back and I let her in. I don't know, but I will not do that anymore. I will just keep giving her to the Lord. I realize now I can do nothing for her at this point except pray. I need to let her go, and I'm choosing to do that at this moment. Lord, I give her to you.

— Cindy

Good work, Cindy!

I'm sure none of that was easy to hear, but like a faithful soldier, you just keep moving forward. I think you understand what I'm saying in regards to your mom, but just in case you missed my point, I wanted to share a quote from Section 2217 of the Catechism: It says, *Obedience toward parents ceases with the emancipation of the children...*

You are no longer obligated to do everything your parents tell you. If your parents order you around, you and your parents are both in sin. You are an adult, and you need to make your own choices and decisions in life. You will also be held accountable before the Lord for everything that happens. You need to bow down in obedience to the Lord, not to earthly humans, parents or other family members.

Passivity is another sin. If you are passive and allow everybody to boss you around and tell you what to do, then your spirit-woman is not standing strong. When you are passive and your spirit-woman is hiding, there will be all kinds of evil influences that will try to push and pull you in a million different directions. When your spirit-woman is strong with the Lord and you are strong in the Lord's armor, then you will be empowered to make decisions for the Lord and help advance his kingdom.

We are required to be respectful to our parents and help them in their old age, but we should never allow them to abuse us or project their evil on us. If your parents are healthy and wise, you can ask their advice, but as an adult, you should never allow them to make decisions on your behalf.

— Rob

Dear Rob,

Things are not good here. I really need prayer. I tried to stand up for what I thought was right, and it turned out really bad. My son and my husband treated me like dirt. My husband used to do this when our daughters were at home. Now it's starting all over again with our teenage son.

My mother is constantly calling, and I'm trying really hard not to take it in. I studied the Catechism and the quote you sent over. For the last three days, I have been reading your words and praying and meditating on everything. I totally understand and agree with all of it.

I've been going through a grieving process for the childhood I never had, and will never have. I just keep giving my mom to the Lord and asking him to break all ties like you said. I have this horrible feeling that something bad is going to happen either to my mom or my dad. I know the Lord is in charge, and I will keep giving them to him.

I'm not taking them back. It's been hard, but I've been doing it. The only reason I even took her calls was that each time, I thought she might be calling about my dad. They don't know if he's had two mini-strokes or if he's trying to have a heart attack. I never took in any of my mom's negativity. She has tried her best to play games with me, but I'm not playing. I just keep giving her to the Lord.

To make matters worse, my son is sick and my husband is tired, so they take it out on me. This has been going on a long time. Today especially, since I'm trying to stand in the light. I tried to stand up for what was right, and they both let me have it. I kept rebuking Satan and calling on the Holy Spirit, but it didn't stop. After all the disrespectful actions and bad words they just walk away when I'm talking. It really makes me feel like a nobody.

At one point I cussed, which I never do, but they hurt me so badly and made me very angry. This is why I usually just keep my mouth shut and stay out of everybody's way. They always win. They just talk down to me, or hang up on me, or walk away from me. I really wanted to work for the Lord, and I really wanted you to think I was ready. It's so hard to tell you this, but I know I have to.

Needless to say, the 40 days are shot. Please don't think bad of me. You couldn't be more disappointed in me than I am in myself. I feel that I will never be able to work for the Lord, and that breaks my heart. Please don't yell at me. I can't take one more person being mad at me today. I know you've really tried to help me, and I really appreciate it. More than anything I want to do God's will. I'm not giving up. I'm just telling you about the day.

— Cindy

Chapter Twenty-Two

Dear Rob,

I'm going back to fasting on the vegetables. I have a broken heart that's bleeding all over the place. I hope the Lord will help me get stronger if I offer him this fast.

Please don't be mad at me for anything. Please don't think bad of my family. It always makes me feel terrible to say anything about them to anybody. I love them with all my heart.

But they really broke me this time. I'm lower than I've ever been.

I have nothing left inside of me that thinks I'm worth anything. It's hard to believe God would want to be with me, or have anything to do with me. I feel so bad for failing him again. It's hard for me to look at him. I feel so ashamed.

— Cindy

Dear Cindy,

I want you to keep fighting. I want to you to continue to stand for the Lord's truth and love in your family. You are the light of Christ. Your house would be complete darkness if it weren't for you. I want you to be loving in the face of their abuse. The more mean and vicious your family is, the more loving, kind and positive I want you to be.

When they call you names, I want you to tell them how much you love them. The next time your mom calls, read her your list of affirmations. I want you to prepare a list of all the loving qualities of your family, and the next time they start verbally abusing you, I want you to get the list and read it to them. If they walk away, follow them. If they run away, read the list the next time you see them.

Romans 12:20 says, *If your enemies are hungry, feed them; if they are thirsty, give them something to drink; for by doing this you will heap burning coals on their heads.*

This is what I want you to do, heap burning coals of love on top of their heads. Your loving words will feel like burning coals, and it will make them see the ugliness of their actions. I also want you to pray the Lord's conviction on all those who verbally abuse you.

The Lord's conviction is a great blessing. Whenever we are in sin and cut off from God, we need the Lord's conviction to help us turn away from sin and repent. If we don't turn away and repent, we will remain cut off from God. Being convicted by the Holy Spirit is a great blessing, because it helps us get back into right relationship with God.

I want you to pray for the Holy Spirit to heap burning coals of conviction upon the heads of anyone who verbally abuses you, and I want you to be loving in the face of their abuse. You are strong enough to do this. If eating more food gives you the strength to be loving in the face of their abuse, then by all means, order several pizzas, write your list and start acting assertively.

You have the power to win this battle. Nothing is more powerful than love. Bring on the light of Christ! Light your lamp of love and let it shine!

— Rob

Dear Rob,

When I opened your e-mail I wondered what you could possibly say to make me feel better. You did it, I feel better. Thank you. This is something I can do, and I will do it.

I also thank you for giving me permission to eat pizza if that's what it takes. If I'm going to make it, I'm going to do it through the power of God. I won't take comfort or strength from false gods anymore. I want everything to be of the Lord. Your permission to eat pizza has only helped strengthen my resolve.

I will do what you say. I will do it for God, and I will do it for my family. I really don't care about doing it for myself. If it was just me, I would go off somewhere alone and never see or talk to anybody again. I've started going to this little church where nobody knows me so I can be invisible. It's like penance, reading those affirmations, but I'll do what you say. I will heap lots of burning coals on all their heads!

— Cindy

Dear Rob,

I have been standing up for God, and a lot of people don't like it. I'm doing exactly what you said, and I'm not sure anybody knows how to take it. I still go and cry alone, but I stay strong and loving in front of them. It seems to be working. It just hurts me when people turn away and don't want to hear the truth.

I have been praying about fasting, and I feel the Lord doesn't want me make another 40-day vegetable fast. He said I could continue to fast from bingeing, but he doesn't want me to do vegetables right now. He wants me to be free to choose good food for him. I felt this so strongly in my heart, like when you gave me permission to eat pizza. Somehow it gave me more strength to choose God over food.

He wants me to be completely free to choose him. He also told me that I'm not to keep starting over. I have claimed the next 40 days for him. I may do 30 of them standing, and ten of them flat on my face. It doesn't matter if I fall; if I get back up, the days still count. He accepts them all.

He also wants all of me just as I am, broken, hurt, beaten up and fallen down. He loves me. He also wants me to start seeing myself as he sees me. That's really hard for me to do, but I'm trying. It's hard to look at myself, because I have never liked myself. I've always hated myself, but I'm realizing that hating myself, is hating God, because he lives in me. As long as I have a breath, I will take it for him.

— Cindy

Dear Cindy,

It's good to hear you are standing strong. I'm also very happy to hear the Lord doesn't want you to start over if you mess up. It sounds like he wants you to learn self-forgiveness and self-love, not how to beat yourself up when you make a mistake.

What kind of medication are you taking?

Can you share a small scene of your family's situation without feeling bad? You said you have been standing up for God and some people don't like it. Who would that be, and what happened? What would happen if you read your list of affirmations to your mother?

— Rob

Dear Rob,

I'm glad you're OK with everything I told you about fasting. It makes me feel I'm discerning correctly when you agree.

I'm taking painkillers and muscle relaxers for my leg. The doctor also prescribed an antidepressant, but I haven't been taking it. I'm not taking the full dose of the other medications either, because if I do, I can't drive myself to Mass in the mornings.

I had a great experience with my family last night. My husband and son both were making jokes at my expense. I started to feel sick and started to leave the room. Then I stopped myself and I tried to joke back. I started saying nice things about them, and did nice things for them. All of the sudden, they had a change of heart and started being nice to me.

In regards to my mother, I will do anything you ask me to do, but please don't ask me to read my affirmations to her. I don't want to share anything with her that means anything to me. I can guarantee you she will find a way to ruin them for me.

It's hard enough to read the affirmations to myself and to believe them. I'm trying to believe they are true. I want them to be true. No, I haven't read them to my family either. I'm basically just killing them with kindness, and it seems to be working.

— Cindy

Dear Cindy,

You write me back and say that you did everything I have asked; yet you are afraid or ashamed to share your affirmations with your family. What's up with that?

In your last letter you said your family was making you the butt of their jokes. Just last week we were talking about honoring our parents. What are you teaching your son if you allow him to dishonor his mother? If you fail to stand up for what is right, then you are helping your son violate the Fourth Commandment. If he grows up learning disrespect, why should he have respect towards any form of authority? Are you starting to see your son disrespect other forms of authority outside your home?

There's a spiritual battle taking place inside your home over your identity. Are you worthless, or are you valuable? Do you believe your affirmations, or are you just placating the author. I asked you to fight for your self-worth. When your family calls you names, I want you to tell them all the reasons why you love them. I want you to make a list of affirmations for all your family members and say them out loud, especially when they are attacking you.

I also want you to start speaking your *own* affirmations when your family members attack you. I want you to put an end to this battle over your identity. Right now, you haven't solved anything. They attack you verbally, you act nice to make them stop, and later you cry from all the pain. This is a battle, and in order to win, you may need to get bloody. Right now, I don't even think you are fighting; it sounds like you are placating.

If I had my way with your family, they would be making a list of 50 affirmations for you, and they would be saying them to you. This is the benchmark for victory. Right now, you are nowhere near any kind of resolution. The next time someone has a bad day, they will take it out on you. Why? Why do you allow this? Why won't you take a stand for your self-worth?

— Rob

Chapter Twenty-Three

Dear Rob,

You're right, I'm sorry. I thought I was doing what you said, but I wasn't. I see that now.

I don't want to placate. I will start saying my affirmations to my family and to my mother. I will stand up for myself and demand the respect, especially from my son, whom I want to be holy, too.

My son is very respectful to authority and a good boy. I think the only reason he hasn't been respectful to me is that he has seen his father and sisters disrespect me. I have taken it from everybody because I thought I deserved it and because I didn't think I had the power to stop it. I see now that I have opened the door and allowed evil to come in and have a party! I have endangered not only my own soul, but the souls of my family.

Either I believe my affirmations, or I don't. If I believe them, then why wouldn't I say them to everybody? I was afraid to say them because they might act as though they didn't believe them, and then somehow that would make them not true. I want them to be true. I see now that the only person who needs to believe them is me. If I believe them, then I no longer have an excuse to binge or hurt myself, or let others hurt me.

I have been playing the victim, instead of the soldier. I've been blaming my family for making me feel bad. As long as I let them make me feel bad, it gives me an excuse to hurt myself. Instead of being a soldier for Christ and fighting the spiritual war that is going on all around me, I have been allowing evil to destroy everything that is sacred to God. How sick is that? Why couldn't I see this before?

This really had nothing to do with my family and everything to do with me. I'm either going to live these affirmations or I'm not. Reading them means nothing if I don't believe them and especially if I don't choose to live them. I'm choosing everything that the affirmations are saying. More importantly, I'm choosing to live them and to proclaim them to everybody!

— Cindy

Dear Cindy,

There are two ways to share your affirmations with your family. If they are attacking you and calling you names, you could fight their lies with the truth. For example, if they call you names, saying things like, "You are stupid and worthless," you could respond with the Word of God: "The Bible says I'm created in the image and likeness of God. I'm a woman of great strength and beauty! I love you, and I'm your mother! Why are you trying to hurt me with your vicious and disrespectful jokes?"

The other way would be to bring your situation into the light and ask for your family's support. You could wait for the right time and approach your family members individually and say, "I would like to ask for your support. I'm trying to lose weight and be healthier. I usually turn to food every time I start feeling bad about myself. When you call me names, it hurts me. When you ignore me and walk away when I'm talking to you, it hurts me.

"Whenever I'm feeling hurt, I turn to food to comfort myself. In an attempt to feel better about myself, I'm practicing affirmations. This list is who I am and who I am striving to be. I would like to share it with you, and I have also made a list of affirmations about all the positive qualities that I love about you."

You may want to tell them about how your mom's negativity has hurt you ever since you were a little girl. You should tell them how much their words hurt you in past arguments and ask for their support in the future.

By bringing this situation into the light and standing strong every time they attack your character, you will win this battle for the Lord. Your family members will not change overnight; they may still get angry and fall back into destructive patterns; but every time you stand in truth and pray for the Lord to show them their guilt, they will change. Little by little, they will stop attacking you and start supporting you. You have the power to completely remove this darkness from your home. You have already been guaranteed victory through Christ!

— Rob

Dear Rob,

I have fought several bloody battles in the last couple of days. The worst was with my son. I asked him to do a simple housecleaning chore. He said no, and gave all kinds of excuses. I stood my ground, with love. He even threw something at me. He finally did what I asked, and then I told him he had to apologize. He did with complete sincerity.

The next battle with him was less bloody, and the next even less. After about seven more battles our relationship is back to normal. I think it was God's providence that my husband wasn't around when all this took place. It was just between my son and me. Our last few conversations have been very respectful and loving.

I also fought the same kind of battles with my husband. I didn't ask him to apologize, but he did anyway. I was put to the test with my three daughters, and I stood my ground with them, too.

All my family members have heard my affirmations, even my mother. She was the biggest foe of all. I really had to stand my ground with her. After realizing I had a choice, it wasn't hard to choose the Lord, and put a stop to evil in all its forms.

I made a choice to be a loving wife and mother, a child of the light, a woman of great strength, a woman of great courage, a woman of great beauty. I'm free to be healthy, to eat good foods and to be loved. I have the right to make mistakes. I have the right to express my true feelings, to be real and loved by my friends. I am Jesus' little white lamb. I'm free to exercise my body, to feel good about myself and to be a soldier for Christ.

— Cindy

Dear Cindy,

Do you remember when you were going to join a gym? What happened to that? I think you should go to the gym three times a week, even if you do nothing but show up. Maybe after a week of going to the gym and watching other people, you could start walking on the treadmill. Surely, your family shouldn't be upset with that.

Going to the gym will help you live your affirmations and help you start taking care of your body. If you are unable to walk because of your leg, you could start with some upper body exercises. How about some lateral pull-downs? You can even start working out from home. Let me know if you are interested, and I will send you more information.

— Rob

Dear Rob,

I have a treadmill. I used to walk on it, but I haven't for a long time. I will again when I can. I'm not supposed to be on my leg any more than necessary. The bone chips needs to dissolve before I can exercise. I guess that could take a long time. I'll also join the gym when I can, because I would like to do the weight machines. I could do some upper body exercises, as you say. Just let me know how, and I will do it.

My father is having a heart test and probably heart surgery on Tuesday. My first thought was that I can't go, for physical reasons, but I have to go. I prayed, and the Lord told me I could go, and that he would go with me.

My mother tried to take control of the situation — whether I come, when I come and how I come. I took back all the control and told her I would be coming after my doctor appointment, and that I would be driving myself. I told her that she needed to get a priest to give my dad the sacrament of the sick, or else I would bring one myself when I arrived.

I will be leaving tomorrow afternoon. I don't know when I'll be returning.

— Cindy

Dear Rob,

I'm still at my parents' house. I'm leaving sometime today to go home. My dad is miraculously OK. After they performed tests at the hospital, they discovered his heart was perfect. He doesn't have to have open-heart surgery after all!

I have so much to tell you. There have been many bloody battles since I got here. I have to tell you up front, I haven't maintained a very healthy diet, but I've experienced great victory at everything else! You can't believe how God has protected me, and how many times I have stood up for him and against Satan and won! I even went so far as to talk to my mom last night about not taking the Lord's name in vain.

Everybody tried to talk me out of going to Mass last night for numerous reasons. I almost caved, but at the last minute, I told them I was going. I told my family I had to go thank God for saving Dad. While I was at Mass, my entire family had a horrible fight. God protected and saved me while I was away. I missed the tornado, and by the time I got back, the storm had cleared.

So this is what it feels like when you stand strong for the Lord. It feels really good! I've never known this kind of strength before.

— Cindy

Dear Rob,

When I was driving home from my parents' house, I felt this huge closeness to the Lord in my heart. It came over me several times. I just couldn't stop telling him how much I loved him. It brought me to tears. It had nothing to do with anything except knowing him and feeling a deep love for him.

This is the first time in my life that I was who God made me to be around my mother. Now that I'm home, I think he is calling me to fast on vegetables again. I'm off those pills. I want God's plan, and I think those pills were hindering me.

I have never had this kind of strength before. Never. Something has happened, and something has changed. I know I'm going to be a witness for him. I already am. That's why I think he is calling me back to fasting.

I need to stay super close to him, especially as all this is happening. Since I didn't take your advice and went back to eating bad foods and Diet Coke, I'm sure I'm going to have a hard time the first few days.

I'm kind of scared to start a 40-day fast again, but I know I'm supposed to. I want to do whatever he wants me to do.

— Cindy

Chapter Twenty-Four

Congratulations, Cindy!

It sounds like you were a true soldier for Christ in your family's world of darkness.

In regards to the fasting: How about a few days on vegetables and water and then go five to seven days on juice and water? The vegetables and water will help clean out the chemicals from your system and prepare you for the juice and water.

I fast on juice and water whenever I need more of the Lord's anointing in my life. When I'm doing healing work, I fast all week on juice and water and ask the Lord to break me and burn all the unhealthy sins, unforgiveness and emotional wounds out of my soul. I call them holy weeks because I spend all week in a church writing healing letters, journaling and practicing imagination techniques.

You can even add some protein powder to your juice once or twice a day. You are not allowed to have any artificial chemicals in your body, so when choosing protein powder, make sure it's pure protein without any appetite suppressing drugs.

Five to seven days will be enough time to get your spirit-woman fired up for the Lord. It will break your food addiction, and on the third day, you will be on a spiritual high. It may make you physically weaker, but the strength in your spirit-woman will make it all worthwhile.

After your fast, all you need to do is go back to a healthy diet. Let's go over the requirements for a healthy diet one more time — no sweets, no chemicals, no soft drinks, no caffeine, no snacking between meals and no eating after 7 p.m. Do you take vitamins? If not, you will need to start taking a good women's formula.

— Rob

Dear Rob,

I'm awfully scared to start fasting again because I haven't been eating very well. My flesh doesn't want to give up the junk food. I have been fighting with myself all day. My flesh wants to eat junk.

Thank you for telling me a second time about a healthy diet. I don't think I was ready to listen before. I am now. I know it's a sin not to take care of my body, because it's a temple of the Holy Spirit. I know my food addiction has held the Lord back from giving me all that he wants and from doing what he wants me to do.

I don't take vitamins, but I will get some. The Diet Coke is going to be the hardest. I'm extremely addicted to it, and there are still a couple cans in the house. I have been looking at them all day, because I wanted to consciously choose the Lord over them. I'm thinking I should pour them down the drain, and I will pray the Lord take away my taste for anything unhealthy.

The fact that he wants me changes everything. I wasn't sure he wanted me before. When I realize he does want me, just the way I am, it's such an incredible joy. I was so messed up in my thinking before. I always thought I had to get holy before he would want me, and yet I couldn't get holy without being with him, so that always kept me away from him, even though my heart always wanted to be with him.

— Cindy

Dear Cindy,

If it makes you feel any better, I will be fasting with you. I'm starting Sunday morning on juice and water and going all week because I need the Lord's anointing. I have a three-day revival service in New Hampshire beginning Monday. I will keep fasting on juice and water through Friday because I need the Lord's anointing to do one-on-one emotional healing appointments all week.

Fasting is extremely powerful. You will be on a spiritual high that far exceeds any fleshly gratification. If I can fast all week to bring the Lord's anointing to others, surely you can fast to bring the Lord's healing into your own life.

Buy some good vitamins and a lot of tomato juice, orange juice and grapefruit juice. If you have a juicer, you can even make fresh carrot juice. Eat a little salt with your tomato juice and drink lots of water.

Beat your flesh into submission. Athletes exercise control in all things. If your flesh starts complaining, give it a quart of grapefruit juice. If it continues whining, give it a half-gallon of water. Keep drinking juice and water and pray like you have never prayed before.

— Rob

Dear Rob,

You're right. I can do this, and I will do this. I will start on Sunday morning with juice and water.

— Cindy

Dear Cindy,

I'm happy to hear you will be fasting with me. Juice and water is the right fast for you. Forty days is way too long. If the Lord isn't calling you to make a 40-day fast, then you won't have the purpose and strength to follow through week after week. Without the Lord's strength and purpose, you will be setting yourself up for failure.

Five to seven days will be over before you know it. Besides, juice and water is the authentic fast of champions. The vegetable fast is good, but you are still eating all the time. Trust me, this is the right fast for you.

I would start getting ready for the fast by seriously cutting down on your food intake and especially by eliminating all sweets, caffeine and chemicals. I don't want you to feel like you are dying on the second day. You are also not allowed to have dairy products on a juice fast. I'm sorry, but milk will be considered cheating.

You probably should tell your family about your intentions and ask for their support. Don't be scared. The Lord will be with you. I'm fully confident the Lord will feed you supernaturally.

During your fast, I would like to ask you to discern the difference between mouth hunger, authentic stomach hunger and fleshly driven hunger.

— Rob

Dear Rob,

I have told my family about the fast, and they are supporting me. That right there is a miracle. I'm already not feeling very good, because I'm on the third day of the vegetable fast. It's my own fault for going back to all the unhealthy foods and chemicals.

Since I'm not feeling well it's hard to focus. I'm even more scared of not eating at all, but I'm going to do it. I will go to the store and get protein powder and a good women's vitamin. Can I drink decaf tea?

As much as my flesh doesn't want to give up the unhealthy foods, I know they are not of the Lord. I know my flesh likes junk food, no getting around it. I want it. I love it. I crave it, but I want God more. I love God more. I crave God more. My heart is burning to know him more intimately.

— Cindy

Dear Cindy,

Decaf tea is good with honey. Just try to avoid juice with sugar, corn sweetener and chemicals. Try to get 100% real juice. Dole makes some refrigerated juice in half gallons, and there is also natural, fresh juice that has not been pasteurized. Also, don't take vitamins on an empty stomach. They will make you feel nauseated. Take them with your protein shake in the morning.

I'm leaving early Monday, and I may not have time to check my e-mail for a few days, although I look forward to hearing about your progress. If you cry out to God during this fast with all your strength, you will encounter the Almighty like never before. Whenever I have embarked on a holy week, God has worked many profound miracles.

— Rob

Dear Rob,

I went to bed early last night because I wasn't feeling very good. My legs kept cramping. I thought if I could get to sleep, I would be OK until morning. Unfortunately, I woke up in the middle of the night shaking, sweating and feeling bad and really scared. It was such a dark and heavy fear I could hardly face it.

Something or somebody kept telling me that I needed to eat something. I kept saying, no, I'm not breaking the fast for the Lord. I got up and wanted to e-mail you, even though I knew you would probably not read it or be able to respond. I ended up going back to bed and I got in the fetal position and started to pray my way through the battle.

I truly believe there was a spiritual war for my soul last night. I've never experienced anything like it. It was like this all night. I had to make a conscious choice to choose God. I was really scared. I just prayed all night and begged God to help me.

This went on for hours. By morning, I slept a little, and when I woke up, I knew it was over. I knew good had conquered evil.

— Cindy

Dear Rob,

I have tremendous gratitude to the Lord for giving me this week. In some ways I feel sad, because I know the grace to continue is leaving me. I don't want to lose this closeness he and I have been feeling.

This morning a friend brought over a fresh-baked apple pie. I had to laugh. The minute the fast has come to completion, Satan's all over me. I have no desire to eat it. My son has friends over, and between them and my husband, it will be gone by morning. It looks like poison to me — a one-way ticket back to the bottomless pit of addiction. I pray with all my being never to go back there again!

— Cindy

Congratulations, Cindy!

You have come a long way! There's a tremendous sense of peace and strength in your writing. It brings me great joy to be a part of your victory. You have completed a seven-day fast on juice and water, and I'm extremely proud of you. You have earned your wings and deserve to be decorated with honors as a soldier of Christ in the army of God.

You have also earned the right to move up in rank. I would like you to ask the Lord if he has a new name that he would like to bestow upon you.

I realize it has been less then six months from the date we first started working together, and that we will need to do a little more healing work, but I think you're ready to enter your calling. How would you like to write a book together? A book to help others come to know Christ!

— Rob

Oh my gosh, Rob!

I have read your letter over and over, and I'm just in shock!

I keep reading it over and over because I can't believe what I'm hearing! Do you know how long I have hoped for something like this? This is so far beyond my wildest dreams! I just can't tell you how in shock I am.

More than anything, I'm grateful to you for so much. You have helped me in so many ways. I don't even know where to start thanking you, and now this!

You just can't know how much this means to me and how incredibly happy and excited I am to even think about writing a book with you. I can't quit crying buckets of grateful tears to you and to God for everything.

I want so much to live my life for God, and to help others. I have always had it in my heart to do something like this, and now you are offering me the opportunity of a lifetime. I just can't believe it. I really just can't believe it.

Never in a million years did I think you would say something like this to me. All of it, the whole letter, every single word just blows me away and makes me cry such tears of joy and gratitude. I hope you know, I have never been so grateful to anyone in my life.

Thank you! Thank you! Thank you!

Steps to Freedom

Make a List of Traumatic Past Experiences

Start by making a list of all your negative past experiences. If you want to be free from your past, you will need to dig down deep in your heart and uncover all the pain. Everything will need to be brought to the light for healing. Don't be afraid. It might hurt, and you might cry a thousand tears, but this is the first step toward healing. Start right now by making a list of the ten worst experiences that you have encountered.

Start Writing Healing Letters

The next step is writing healing letters. This technique will help you vent all your negative emotions and replace them with the love and support you needed, but never received. A list of instructions for the Healing Letter Exercise can be found on page 283. Start your healing process today by writing your first healing letter.

Practice Positive Affirmations

To start practicing positive affirmations, all you need to do is replace your negative internal dialogue with a list of positive qualities about yourself. Start right now by writing a list of twenty-five items, such as, *I am kind, honest, intelligent, beautiful, loyal and trustworthy. I'm created in the image and likeness of God. God loves me and has a purpose and plan for my life.*

Repeat your list of affirmations over and over to yourself until you start seeing yourself as God sees you. God is loving, kind, compassionate, peaceful, wise, strong, courageous and trustworthy. You have all these characteristics as well, because you were created in the image and likeness of God.

Breaking Vows and Agreements with Evil

All sin is an agreement with evil. Every time we commit sin, we are saying no to God, and yes to evil. Once a pattern of sin has been established, the presence of darkness can acquire a foothold in your life. For example, a gambling addiction might start out as entertainment, but when combined with the sin of greed, a thrill-seeking activity can quickly turn into an obsession.

After a gambler has lost his house, marriage, and all the money in his children's bank accounts, he might want to quit, but if he has made agreements with the presence of evil, the demonic influence that is driving his behavior will not let him go, unless the vows and agreements are broken.

Oftentimes, we don't even know we are making vows with evil, but once these legal contracts are made, they are very difficult to uncover and break. The enemy doesn't want you to uncover the lies and agreements, because it is through these vows that the presence of darkness has access to your life, soul and compulsive behaviors.

You will need the power of the Holy Spirit to uncover and break all the vows that are keeping you held in an addiction cycle. You will need to ask God to shine the light of his Holy Spirit into your heart and disclose all sinfulness, lies and distorted perceptions. Once these devices are uncovered, simply ask for the Lord's forgiveness and break them in Jesus' name.

Start Fasting for the Lord

Fasting is an extremely powerful way to open the floodgates of God's grace. When a man fasts, he is not punishing himself or inflicting pain on his body in an attempt to please God. Fasting is denying the physical need for food in exchange for spiritual food. When a man fasts, he is converting his fleshly hunger into spiritual hunger. When he cries out to God with spiritual hunger, God will answer his cry and feed him supernaturally.

You can start today by skipping one meal. Make sure you drink a lot of water and then convert all your food hunger into God hunger. After you have acquired the ability to skip one meal, increase the length of your fast to a full day. Make sure you drink a lot of juice and water and cry out to God with all your strength. After you have acquired the ability to fast all day, increase your fast to three days and then try a full week.

On the third day, you will experience God's presence like never before. Fasting will break all strongholds that evil has on your life and will make room for the Lord to come into your heart. Fasting is an extremely powerful way to hear from the Lord and eliminate all your compulsive behaviors.

Surrender Your Life to the Lord

God created you with an incredible purpose and plan for your life. You can be your own god, or you can surrender your life to the Lord and ask for his leadership and guidance in all your endeavors.

When you surrender your life and free will to the Lord, he will send the power of his Holy Spirit to dwell in your heart. The God of the universe will adopt you as his own beloved child, and the Almighty will begin the process of fixing all the mistakes you have made with your life.

God is waiting for your complete surrender. He loves you and wants you to surrender your life, obedience and free will into his hands. Ask him to restore your life and take you on an exciting adventure. There is nothing to fear. Surrender everything to him so that he can transform you into a new creation in Christ.

Invite Christ into Your Heart

Jesus is standing at the door of your heart, knocking and waiting. The Lord wants you to open the doors of your heart, so that he can come in and be with you. He wants you to make room for him by healing all your emotional wounds and surrendering all your self-willed ways. When you do, the Spirit of Jesus will enter your heart, and you will be forever free — free to be the child of God the Lord intended you to be.

Healing Letter Exercise

1. Spend some time in Adoration chapel and ask the Lord to show you the situation he wants you to work on next.

2. After you identify a hurtful event that needs healing, try to separate the situation from everything else that has happened to you. For example, if you grew up with a critical father, instead of trying to work through years of emotional abuse in one letter, try to identify one experience when your father hurt you the most.

3. Begin the exercise from a prayerful and meditative state of mind. Find a quiet place where you can be alone with the Lord. Make sure you have plenty of tissues and the necessary writing supplies.

4. Picture the person who hurt you in your imagination. Imagine he can hear everything you are about to say to him. If the person is deceased, picture him in heaven standing next to Jesus.

5. Begin writing your letter with the words, *Dear Dad, I'm angry because you hurt me!* Tell this person all the ways that he has hurt you by his careless and disrespectful actions. Keep writ-

ing the words *I'm angry,* over and over again. Vent all your anger on paper. Don't worry about spelling or grammar; just say everything you need to say.

6. After you vent all your anger, move on to any fears that you may have experienced. How has this person affected your life? Describe how his careless behaviors have carried forward into your present-day relationships. Describe how the sins of the father have been passed down to the third and fourth generations.

7. After you vent any fears or guilty feelings, get in touch with your sadness. Tell this person what you wanted to happen that didn't. If you're writing to your father say, *I'm sad because I wanted a better father. I'm sad because I wanted you to love me. I wanted you to treat me like a beloved daughter. I wanted your love and support.*

8. Conclude your letter with anything else you need to say to this person, and then begin a new letter by picturing the person who hurt you in a completely healed state. Picture them in heaven standing next to Jesus. Imagine this person full of God's love. Because they are full of God's love, they now want to apologize to you.

9. Start your imaginary response letter by saying, *Dear daughter, I'm sorry. I'm sorry for hurting you. You didn't deserve to be treated like that. I'm so sorry. Please forgive me.*

10. It doesn't matter if this person would apologize to you or not. This is your healing letter, and you have the right to give yourself the loving words that you deserve to hear. Do not allow another person's hardness of heart to interfere with your

forgiveness process. Write down all the words that you deserve to hear.

11. Conclude your response letter with prayer. Release the person who hurt you into the Lord's hands. Ask Jesus to wash away any demonic filth that you may have picked up by accepting this person's abuse. Ask Jesus to bind up all the demons and have them destroyed in the lake of fire. Surrender this person to the Lord and if appropriate, ask Jesus to break all unhealthy soul-ties.

12. Allow Jesus to speak to you through a closure letter. Accept the Lord's love and forgiveness. Allow the Lord's love and forgiveness to flow into your heart and cleanse you of all curses, resentment and negativity. Ask the Lord to show you if there's anything else you need to release. Allow yourself to fall into the Lord's arms and be permanently set free — free to be the child of God the Lord intended you to be.